# MR. PARSONS PRESENTS ALL THE THREE LETTER WORDS

## BY

## TANNER PARSONS

authorHOUSE

1663 LIBERTY DRIVE, SUITE 200
BLOOMINGTON, INDIANA 47403
(800) 839-8640
www.authorhouse.com

*First published by AuthorHouse 07/06/04*

*ISBN: 1-4184-7014-7 (sc)*

*Library of Congress Control Number: 2004094596*

*Printed in the United States of America*
*Bloomington, Indiana*

*This book is printed on acid-free paper.*

for all my students

"Never let schooling interfere with your education."

Mark Twain

# Foreword

As obsessions go, this puppy is unique.

Motivated by nothing familiar to me, Mr. Parsons is delivering a dictionary of three-letter words. My mission, it only follows, is to attempt an introduction without those very creatures, if only to emphasize their importance in this nation's daily rituals.

Imagine please, what's unavailable to me: Essential articles. Crucial possessives & pronouns. Several elementary numbers. Vital conjunctions. Obnoxious crossword-puzzle filler. Every last word in that seven word slogan employed by Dumas' trio of Musketeers.

Mr. Parsons' point? A love affair with this gallery of bite-size morsels? A devotion to triptychs? A fixation on their muscular, triangular symmetry? I have no clue. What power do three-lettered words possess that is unavailable to their four-letter cousins?

Perhaps each question will be answered, this mystery solved when we reach obsession's final stanza. Maybe no such closure is possible. Whatever this teacher's case, enjoy this earnest effort. Embrace familiar friends; introduce yourself to this gallery of novel three-letter combinations. Never again will we breeze by these simple oddities without a second glance.

Steve Duin

April 2004

My name is Mr. Parsons and this class is an overview of all the one, two, and three-letter words. Let's start with attendance. Raise your hand if you are here.

These are the class rules: Whatever rules apply to the room you are truly in trumps anything we agree on in this paragraph. You can chew gum, listen to music, daydream, not finish the assignment, talk to your neighbor, talk back to the author, roll your eyes, and even fail to understand. My main objective is to have a good time.

Why a book about all the little words? I want students to spell correctly but I also want students to know what words mean. Yep. I do. Over the years I have learned that meaning is actually more important than spelling. When I give vocabulary tests, I say the meaning aloud instead of the word. I try to make it easy. For example, if love is a vocabulary word for the week, during the test I say, "This word has four letters, has a silent e, is an emotion stronger than like, and rhymes with dove." The students write l-o-v-e.

Easy sneezy.

I enjoy filling the vocabulary list with easy-to-spell words so students can focus on learning definitions. But I have wasted a lot of time trying to find obscure three-letter words because the best source for all the small words is the dictionary. In the dictionary, the puny words are mixed in with all the long words. So one day, during standardized testing, I grabbed the thickest dictionary in the classroom in order to list all the petite words. It was THE WORLD BOOK DICTIONARY from 1987. It is 2430 pages long and is actually two books! There's A-K and L-Z! They're heavy. I'm tired from carrying them around since the late nineteen nineties.

Why did it take so long to list all the tiny words? In between searching, I got married, had a couple of kids, bought a house, moved all the furniture in, sold it, moved all the furniture out, quit teaching, moved to Oregon, finished a different book, did some gardening, wrote some poems, and had laser eye surgery.

But wait! It is always better to use more than one source. I needed another dictionary. But my hands were full with the two large books and the two small children. So, I gently dropped everything, went online to Bartleby.com, and found THE AMERICAN HERITAGE DICTIONARY OF THE ENGLISH LANGUAGE, FOURTH EDITION. That's when my headache began. Allow me to confoundedly explain overly much.

As near as I can figure, our main reference, THE WORLD BOOK DICTIONARY, lists all the words in the English language, except curse words. This dictionary even lists words in English that are used in Australia, England, South Africa, Scotland, and more. That explains the heaviness! On the other hand, THE AMERICAN HERITAGE DICTIONARY OF THE ENGLISH LANGUAGE, FOURTH EDITION, is less than half the length of THE WORLD BOOK DICTIONARY. It focuses on English words used in the United States only. So, there are plenty of teensy-weensy words which are in one but not both dictionaries.

Common words like yes, cup, hog, and zit are clearly bona fide words and need no further clarification.

Obscure words like moa, sny, sib, gad, and yew? If both dictionaries include them, I either refer to them as bona fide words or make no distinction. No distinction means it is bona fide. Any word that is NOT in both dictionaries is noted.

There are lots of tiny words in this book you are holding that come from Scotland. Do not use them in Scrabble or Boggle.

If a word was used in a play by Shakespeare centuries ago, it is in THE WORLD BOOK DICTIONARY. Many of these old words are noted in THE WORLD BOOK DICTIONARY as archaic and my book also uses that term.

I exclude abbreviations. There are so many, they warrant their own silly book. Some abbreviations have evolved into words and they are discussed. I do include a few abbreviations simply because I like them.

I include a whole lot of names because I like them, also. Many of the names were discovered simply by writing three simple letters into Google's search engine. In case an entry was both a word and a name, the word trumped the name.

There is a special code that some people use when writing instant messages, emails, and other notes. "Why are you in trouble?" can be written as "Y r u n trouble?" I believe there will be changes in future dictionaries because the people writing this way will one day be working for dictionary publishers. But my silly book does not delve into these waters. Okay, maybe it does a little.

If you think you are in the wrong class, see me afterward.

Any questions?

# All The One Letter Words

We begin with **a**. It can be pronounced as a long vowel or a short vowel. If only more words were as simple and flexible.

**I** think we are off to a good start.

Francis Scott Key originally scribbled out "**O**, say can you see..." The first lyric to *The Star Spangled Banner* is printed today as both "O" and "Oh". It's not only an interjection. "O" can mean nothing without being a zero! Bonus bizarreness: At the beginning of the national anthem this one letter is sung as two syllables.

Prince had hits with *Take Me With **U**, I Would Die 4 U*, and *U Got The Look*. It's not a bona fide word...yet, but the special code of ez writing will create changes in the English Language.

# All The Two Letter Words

When lava cools, it becomes **aa**. It is light and brittle.

**Ab** is the name of a month in the Jewish calendar. But THE WORLD BOOK DICTIONARY does not consider "ab" a word despite the following argument. When exercising, many people work on their abdominal muscles. A slang term for these stomach muscles is abs. Since the muscles are grouped together in your gut, they are nearly always referred to in the plural. Logic dictates that if you have the plural, you can have the singular, ab. THE AMERICAN HERITAGE DICTIONARY OF THE ENGLISH LANGUAGE, FOURTH EDITION, understands and includes this entry.

An advertisement is an **ad**.

The Scottish word for one is **ae**.

There is an animal called an **ai**. I kid you not. It is a three-toed sloth. I'm just realizing this should have been a picture book.

**Al** Franken is a funny man.

I **am** having a good time and hope you are, too.

Do you remember to use **an** in front of nouns that begin with a vowel? Good, but remember, there are exceptions!

BOTH dictionaries I am using include **ar** as an entry. It is bona fide! They argue it is an alternative spelling for "are". Your English teacher won't let you get it away with it. Nor will any of your other teachers. Aaargh!

How we use words is **as** important as the words we use.

**At** first you weren't so sure about this book, but you're warming up to it, eh?

**Au** is a French word but not an English one.

Do you remember Ab is a month in the Jewish calendar? **Av** is another way to spell and say it.

We say **aw** when things don't go our way.

In 1978, at the American Community Schools of Athens, Greece, I got to play the Scarecrow in our high school production of The Wizard of Oz. Dorothy and I were attempting to convince the Tin

Man to join our quest. He asked, "Do you think the Wizard would give me a heart?" I replied, "You bet your **ax**."

The interjection **ay** can mean yes or always.

In ancient Egypt, **ba** is the soul.

"To **be** or not to be" is a famous quote written by William Shakespeare for his character, Hamlet.

Yes, **bi** is a word and not just an abbreviation. Hmmm, how do I discuss its meaning? Pass the buck. Good idea. Ask your parents.

**Bo** Reis was a childhood friend. Where is he now?

*Wonderful World*, sung **by** Elvis Presley, is my favorite song.

THE WORLD BOOK DICTIONARY says **ca** is a Scottish word while THE AMERICAN HERITAGE DICTIONARY OF THE ENGLISH LANGUAGE, FOURTH EDITION, gives it as an abbreviation for "circa" but does not use a period on it. Do not use it in Scrabble. From here to the end of the book, I am shortening our number two reference to just THE AMERICAN HERITAGE DICTIONARY. Think of the ink we'll save.

I played on a softball team in Hollywood, California called the **CV** Shots. We agreed to never divulge what CV stood for. Keeping this vow has been easy because I never knew what it meant.

**Cy** Young won 511 games as a baseball pitcher. No one will catch him. To catch him would mean winning twenty games a season for more than twenty-five seasons.

An informal word for father is **da**. In Burma, a short sword with a heavy back is a da. The weapon can be also be d-a-h.

This one, **de**, is a preposition meaning "from".

Remember the musical scale of do-re-mi? There is a note between do and re called **di**.

**Do** you think this book will catch on?

I love Cirque **du** Soleil.

Long ago, in Babylon, **Ea** was a god of wisdom and water.

Mister **Ed** was the talking horse on television in the sixties.

THE WORLD BOOK DICTIONARY says that eye is **ee** in Scotland. THE AMERICAN HERITAGE DICTIONARY does not see eye to eye with this one and excludes it.

Again they don't come together. THE WORLD BOOK DICTIONARY says "f" is "f" but THE AMERICAN HERITAGE DICTIONARY says the sixth letter is **ef**. Now, stop fighting.

An interjection for not hearing is **eh**. It is usually followed with a question mark.

More controversy! THE WORLD BOOK DICTIONARY says that the letter L is spelled e-l-l. THE AMERICAN HERITAGE DICTIONARY claims it is spelled simply e-l. Either way, both agree that an **el** is an elevated railroad. The lesson we will take from the differences between dictionaries is that English is a malleable language, not a concrete one.

A unit of pica pipe is an **em**. This is also how to spell "m". You already knew about Auntie Em, right?

Half the length of an em is an **en**. I am not making this up. This is also how to spell "n".

My mom's friend Evelyn goes by **Ev**.

Besides being a prefix for hundreds of words, **ex** can stand on its own as the word for "x" and some other meanings as well.

On the do-re-mi musical scale, **fa** is the fourth note.

Do you know the song *Dance The Kung Fu*? Our main reference has an entry for **fu** but our back-up does not. Phooey.

THE WORLD BOOK DICTIONARY has entries for **Ga** and **Ge** having to do with people outside of North America but our American dictionary does not.

Usually we skip the abbreviations but, to honor my dad and to support our troops, the abbreviation of "government issue" gets in. **GI** has become synonymous with soldier. Also, my friend Chuck Martinez likes to wear a gi while practicing martial arts. This is not a bona fide word yet.

The **Go**-Go's are a great 80's band.

**Ha** is a powerful interjection.

A blind man named Al Hibbler had a hit song named **He** in 1955.

At a *Star Trek* convention, I heard Patrick Stewart discuss the differences between **hi** and hello. He basically said that hello suggests more possibilities. The crowd ate it up.

Both reference dictionaries have plenty to say about **ho** but neither mention that it's what Santa Claus chortles.

**Hy** Money is a very successful British photographer.

**I'd** love it if you read this whole book.

Sigmund Freud invented this word. The **id** is a noun referring to our unconscious. Hey, you in the back row, quit reading *The Wizard of Id* and pay attention.

Oops. We forgot to recite *The Pledge of Allegiance*. Should we go back? **If** we do not, am I in trouble? When I taught fifth graders, I was too busy going over the homework and always skipped it. My fault. About once a year, someone would come up and ask why we missed *The Pledge*. I asked the student if he or she was feeling disloyal to the United States in any method or fashion. They always said no. Did they know of anyone who was plotting anything against our great country? They never did. I told the inquisitive student that if they were feeling disloyal at any point during the school day, to let me know, and we would review *The Pledge of Allegiance*.

**I'm** happy you got this far.

Such a busy word! **In** can be a preposition, adjective, adverb, a noun, even a verb. Then it goes on to be a prefix for forty-nine pages of words in THE WORLD BOOK DICTIONARY!

Zeus, the god from Greek mythology, sometimes loved mortals. One of them was **Io**. Io is also the name of Jupiter's largest moon.

Our entry for **is**? In 1944, there was a hit by Louis Jordan called *Is You Is Or Is You Ain't My Baby*. Never heard it but the title sounds fun.

Call <u>**It**</u> Courage by Armstrong Sperry is one of my favorite books to read aloud to students. My classes always love it.

**Iz** is the performing name of the late Israel Kamakawiwa, a Hawaiian musician.

An endearing term for your sweetheart is **jo**.

The ancient Egyptians used **ka** to refer to the soul. THE AMERICAN HERITAGE DICTIONARY leaves this one out.

A Spanish word! A French word! In English, **la** is the sixth note after do, re, mi, fa, and sol. La is also an interjection.

In China, a **li** measures out to about a third of a mile. Both dictionaries include it. It is pronounced like the name Lee.

Did you know **lo** is a bona fide word suggesting surprise?

Khanh **Ly** is a Vietnamese singer.

I sometimes call my mom, **ma**.

Classic narcissistic joke. The speaker talks and talks about himself until he gets tired. Then he says to his friend, "Enough about **me**, what do you think of me?"

The music scale of do-re-**mi** that we keep coming back to has a fancy name. It's called the diatonic scale. Whoa.

THE WORLD BOOK DICTIONARY says **mo** is an informal name for mustache in Australia and since Australia is not in America, that must be why THE AMERICAN HERITAGE DICTIONARY shaves it off.

Both dictionaries except **mu** as the twelfth letter of the Greek alphabet but THE WORLD BOOK DICTIONARY adds that Mu is a mythical lost continent that sunk into the Pacific Ocean at the same time the Atlantic Ocean swallowed up Atlantis. **My** my, learn something new everyday.

**Na** is a Scottish word for **no**. I use it too!

**Ng** is a common Vietnamese last name.

The thirteenth letter of the greek alphabet is **nu**. No lost continents with this one.

A German naturalist named Reichenbach came up with the idea of **od**. I wish he was here to explain it to you but he died in 1869. THE AMERICAN HERITAGE DICTIONARY has an entry for Od, notice the capital, which has to do with an archaic promise.

Kenzaburo **Oe** is Japanese writer who won the Nobel Prize for literature in 1994.

**Of** is pronounced uv. Why can't we spell it that way?

I'm not going to count but I bet that **oh** is the interjection used most often.

This one started as a joke! I just learned from THE WORLD BOOK DICTIONARY that **OK** began as an abbreviation for "oll korrect" which is the wrong way to spell "all correct". THE AMERICAN HERITAGE DICTIONARY uses more than two hundred words describing this entry's delightful history. It can also be written "O.K." and has evolved into the word "okay".

A three letter word that needs shortening? Well, **ol'** is sometimes short for old.

The **Om** is a river in Russia. In the Hindu and Buddhist religions, om, pronounced with a long "o", is a sacred syllable.

I had hoped that these first two chapters would be short and we could get **on** with the true heart of the book but the two letter words keep coming even when we avoid the abbreviations!

Our main reference accepts **oo** as a variant of "oh". THE AMERICAN HERITAGE DICTIONARY does not.

The WBD accepts **op** as an adjective for the term "op art" but The AHD does not let it stand alone. Should we continue just using abbreviations for our references? No! Abbreviations will be dealt with in another book! You in the third row with the apple, go find more vats of ink!

I saw U2 live in Phoenix on Thanksgiving of 2001. How good are they? They can play a boatload of songs to fulfill the audience without playing their biggest hit, *With or Without You.* Who else can do that?

A bone, a mouth, and an esker. Both dictionaries accept **os** as a noun with three definitions. I am as surprised as you are.

THE WORLD BOOK DICTIONARY does not include **ow** as an interjection of pain but THE AMERICAN HERITAGE DICTIONARY does! It is usually followed by an exclamation point.

Ow! An **ox** just stepped on my foot.

A grandchild to someone who speaks Spanish is an **oy** which can also be spelled o-y-e. This is also true in Scotland! But it is not a bona fide word in English.

If they remake *The Wizard of Oz*, Ozzie Smith should play the wizard. Oh, you think it should be Ozzy Osbourne. Well, perhaps we could have a two-headed wizard! You see? Compromise is not so difficult.

Does anyone still refer to their dad as **pa**?

You want to go out to P.E.? But we don't do that until the end of the E entries in the three letter word section. In the meantime, **pe** is the seventeenth letter of the Hebrew alphabet.

The sixteenth letter of the Greek alphabet is **pi**.

Poor is sometimes shortened to **po'**.

Momei **Qu** is a nationally ranked tennis player from Portland, Oregon.

In ancient Egypt, the sun god was **Ra**.

The second note in the do-re-mi scale, I mean, the diatonic scale, is **re**, pronounced like the word ray.

Ensign **Ro** Laren is a *Star Trek* character portrayed by Michelle Forbes.

Both of our reference dictionaries include **sh** as a word even though it lacks a vowel. Synonyms include "quiet", "knock it off", "shush", and "hush". Some teachers are so crafty, they only have to stare at you. Others scream. I've tried every which way but the truth is, I'm usually the one talking.

Besides being yes in Spanish, **si** has at least one musical definition in English.

Peter Gabriel's album **So** is a good one.

An informal way to thank someone in England is to say **ta**.

**Te**, with the capital T that is pronounced as a dee, has a meaning in both Taoism and another in Confucianism.

Do-re-mi-fa-sol-la and **ti**. Those are the seven notes of the diatonic scale. Originally, ti was si, but it was changed in order to be distinct from sol. Plus, a ti is a shrub in Asia.

There is no perfect trick to teach the differences between **to**, too, and two. But, to write well, you need to learn them.

A Spanish word for you is **tu**.

Sure, there was **Ty** Cobb, but there was also Ty Cline, and in the 1970 playoffs, he hit a pinch-hit triple to help put the Cincinnati Reds into the World Series.

Use **uh** whenever you wish to sound confused or uncertain.

**Um**...I have a class discussion each year regarding the usage of the interjection "um". We have a great time becoming aware of how almost everyone in the class starts anything they are about to say with "um".

These days, everyone is down with something. Well, I want to be **up**. Are you up with that?

It is grammatically impossible to begin a sentence with **us**.

Can you believe **ut** is a word? Yep, it sure is. Look it up.

In the Old Testament, the story of Job is set in **Uz**.

Deep in the mountains of northeastern Burma, there is a tribe called **Wa**. Do not mess with them. I mean it.

**"We** the People, of the United States," includes all citizens, not just the wealthiest, the most pious, or the loudest.

The word **wo** is an alternative archaic spelling of woe.

David **Wu** is a congressman from Oregon. Frank Wu is an artist of Science Fiction and Fantasy. The boy in the back row with the headphones on is listening to Wu-tang.

The fourteenth letter of the Greek alphabet is **xi**.

**Ya** is not a word? But my mom says it all the time! And the Rolling Stones had a live album that had to do with getting out one's ya-yas. Plus, there is that sisterhood movie. But NO, both of our reference dictionaries bypass this one.

In movies of old England, there are signs hanging that say "**ye** olde pub" or "ye olde CD shop". I thought ye was an archaic form of "you". I was right, but in the case of the signs, ye is an archaic form of "the". That was the first time I ever ended a sentence with "the". Hey, did it again.

Some people say hi. Some say hello. Still others say **yo**.

There is an all-girl rock band in Florida called **Ze** Bond.

Lao **Zi** was a Chinese philosopher who lived about 2500 years ago. There are a variety of ways to spell his name.

Aargh! Can't get out of the two letter words without a mess. Our main reference says **zo** is a noun that equals "zobo" but our back-up has no zo or zobo. I heard a rumor that a zo is a cross between a cow and a yak and can be written as dzo, dso, zho and dzho! Enough! Help me out by turning the page!

# All The Three Letter Words

A

You've seen pictures of Arabs and some of them will be wearing a sleeveless, heavy-looking, outer garment. That's an **aba**.

Honest **Abe** was a nickname for Abraham Lincoln.

The events at **Abu** Ghraib remind us to treat everyone with dignity, even prisoners of war.

Trouble! Spelling difficulties! Quarreling dictionaries! The entry of **aby** can either be a-b-y or a-b-y-e. It means to pay the penalty. Perhaps it only means that in England because THE AMERICAN HERITAGE DICTIONARY does not list either of these spellings.

In baseball, an **ace** is your best pitcher.

I wanted to be an actor. That happened. I wanted to get paid to **act**. That did not happen very often but I did make some car payments with acting money I made from a TV show called *Dumb Criminals*. I never saw the show. I portrayed a policeman, in case you were wondering.

Did you know **add** comes from the Latin? What does "from the Latin" mean? Well, find Latin on the map and then I will explain.

This word should have been listed as archaic because one only hears it in old plays. The word is **ado** and William Shakespeare used it quite a bit.

An **adz** is a timber shaping tool.

A Scottish preposition and adverb that means off is **aff**. THE AMERICAN HERITAGE DICTIONARY left aff off its pages.

Near the stern is the **aft**. What's a stern? In the book <u>Magic Time</u> by Marc Zicree, the bad guy is named Stern.

A title for respect is **aga**, especially in Turkey.

Many people believe that **age** is a state of mind.

Awhile **ago**, I had a wacky idea about writing a book with all the three letter words. Now, the laundry is backed up.

**Aha**! We've come to great word! It means joy, surprise, or declaration of triumph! All in three letters! Wait, there's more! Sometimes this little booger gets a hyphen between the second and third letters. There was a band named a-ha (yes, with lower case letters) that had a number one song in the 80's. It was called *Take On Me*. My favorite a-ha song is the theme to a James Bond movie called *Living Daylights*.

As you can tell, I sometimes get off topic. If you will forgive me, I'll try not to let it happen again. Who am I kidding? I do it in the next paragraph! I am going to run ahead and simply count the times I go off on a tangent. Let's see, if you'll forgive that last one, we'll call this next one the first one.

Teacher's First Tangent

Introducing the word **ahi**. Before the definition is set forth, let's see if we can come up with our own meaning. Ahi ought to mean that moment just before someone smiles or laughs and they stop themselves. Instead of saying the long-winded sentence of "You nearly smiled right there. I saw that you were about to admit you were having a good time but no, Mr. Grumpy Bear, you have to keep that sullen expression you always carry around," one could simply say "You did an ahi." The word actually comes from Hawaii and is a synonym for a bluefin tuna.

An **ahu** is a raised platform at a Polynesian temple site. THE AMERICAN HERITAGE DICTIONARY does not recognize this entry.

If you don't know what **aid** means...get some help.

The person you get help from might ask, "What ails you?" **Ail** means distress.

Once I saw a sign next to a toilet that said, "We **aim** to please, so you aim too, please."

What is **ain**? No, it is not the prefix for "ain't". According to THE WORLD BOOK DICTIONARY, it is another Scottish word for "one". But according to THE AMERICAN HERITAGE DICTIONARY, it is the Scottish word for "own". Oye.

You know **air**.

But what about **ait**? It was used in England to describe a small island in a river or a lake. Now everybody just points.

The word **aku** describes a fish related to the ahi.

There are three definitions for the word **ala**! It's a wing. It is also one of the cartilages of the nose. Don't start pickin' because I called attention to it. It is also one of two side petals of any flower shaped like the sweet pea. It is also a synonym for armpit. Doesn't that make four definitions?

Did you know that the white linen robe worn by Catholic priests at the Communion Service is called an **alb**?

Beer is a fun word. It does not appear in this book since it is a four letter word. Instead, we'll have something like beer, a little more bitter and a little more intoxicating. We'll have **ale**.

**Alf** was born on the planet Melmac.

"Float like a butterfly and sting like a bee" is poetry from Muhammad **Ali**.

**All** means a lot of things but it is best used as a reminder at the end of *The Pledge of Allegiance*.

When **alp** begins with a lower case "a", it can refer to any high mountain. When there is a capital, it means a single peak of the Alps, which is a major mountain range in Europe.

A noun that represents the first octave above the treble staff is called an **aft**. I don't understand this definition either.In Japan, a woman pearl diver is called an **ama**. Our back-up reference says "ama" is a different form of "amah" which is a housemaid in Portugal. Such a span!

In France, another word for friend is **ami**. But since it is French word, it is not in THE AMERICAN HERITAGE DICTIONARY. Can't use it in Scrabble or Boggle.

Audiophiles love this word; **amp**. It wasn't a word until amplifiers were invented. Amps were invented to boost the level and the quality of sound.

THE WORLD BOOK DICTIONARY says that an **amt** is the largest local administrative unit of Denmark. THE AMERICAN HERITAGE DICTIONARY does not have it as an entry. There will be no test question referring to this one.

**Amy** Tan is a very successful writer. So far, her biggest hit is The Joy Luck Club.

**Ana** is a name but it is also a common noun. A collection of memorable sayings is an ana. A variation on this is a set of things that are connected to a person or a place.

Most English teachers remind students to not begin sentences with **and** and they remind students not to have run on sentences and I am here to remind you that there are plenty of published writers who not only begin sentences with "and" and make it sound fine, but many of those same writers go on and on in one sentence and it makes for wonderful reading.

Another Scottish word for one is **ane**.

Have you ever seen an **ani**? It is a North American bird that is something of a cuckoo with black feathers.

I love my Aunt Betty **Ann**.

**Ano** is a band in Hawaii.

If an **ant** has eight legs, is it related to the octopus?

Got **any** gum?

When ants find food, they go **ape**.

If you put a period on this entry, it will be the abbreviation for apartment. Without the period, **apt** means likely or right for the occasion.

**Apu** always cracks me up.

An **ara** is a noun meaning macaw. Not knowing what macaw meant, I looked it up! It is a certain kind of parrot in Central and South America. Never too old to learn!

Teacher Tangent #2

Hold out your hand like you're about to shake hands. Curve it up and make a rainbow shape. That's an **arc**. It sounds exactly like "ark" but we're not there yet. You are reading this book in order aren't you? If you feel guilty for not reading a book by starting at the beginning, let it go. When a person picks up a book, they fiddle with it, flip the pages, and some folks read the ending first! It is a small percentage of books that are read in order from the title page to the ending. Think of every book as a reference book. Even if we do read a whole book in order, we often go back and reread sections out of order. Our brains can handle it.

A plow is a fairly primitive machine. Alas, there is something more primitive than a plow and that is an **ard**.

The irregular plural of am is **are**.

Neither dictionary has **arf** but I bet a dog's dictionary does. Plus, I bet it's a really short book with hardly more than ruff, bow-wow, and grrr.

I'm looking forward to **Ari** Fleischer's tell-all book.

Is there an **ark** other than Noah's? Can't think of any. They were obsolete before photography was invented, which is why there are no real pictures of arks. If this bothers you, perhaps you can create a "Bring Back The Ark" web site.

To figuratively twist someone's **arm**, is to talk them into your idea.

This is my **art**.

Cinders are small leftover burnt pieces from a fire. Even tinier than a cinder is an **ash**.

**Ask**. If you are going to succeed in this world, you'll have to ask questions.

In Africa and in Europe, an **asp** is a type of poisonous snake. The cobra, for example, is an asp. It is also old poetic short form for aspen, which are trees. We could start a poem about an asp climbing an asp and have fun rhyming with clasp and gasp.


Teacher Tangent #3

We have come to a controversial word. Now, I could simply put it in and explain that it means mule or donkey but that would mean the word would be in print. Appearing in print means that some young children might read and utter the word inappropriately. Can't have that. So, in order for this fantastic piece of literature to be available to the highest number of buyers, er, I mean readers, some words will be left out and I thought it would be far better to have this long explanation rather than a blank page where the word is skipped. A blank page would allow someone to come in and actually write the word down and draw a picture or two. I doubt seriously that anyone would draw a mule or donkey. Writing an inappropriate word is nearly as bad as saying it. So, let's be pleased with ourselves that we've skipped over the conflict completely. You can carry on without feeling besmirched and I can hand the book over to libraries and boldly announce that no nasty language is present. Of course, it's early. These are only the A's. There may be expletives ahead. I happen to KNOW they are in the sequel, which is entitled <u>Mr. Parsons Presents All the Four Letter Words</u>. In that book, I simply must use foul language. If I were to begin cutting out all the inappropriate four-letter words, that book might not get past page one!

Where were we? Yes, the mule/donkey synonym. Let's move on.

This is a classic joke for primary children. Why was Six scared? Because Seven **ate** Nine.

Neither reference I am using includes **auf**. But, on a lark, I found it at brainydictionary.com. Where the heck did they get it?

In the arctic regions, there is a diving sea bird that has its legs set far back on its body and sits like a penguin. Have you ever seen an **auk**?

Teacher Tangent #4
The next entry is **aux**. It is a French word, pronounced in its entirety as a long "o". It means "to the", "at the", and "with the". Why are foreign words in an English dictionary? It is because in the USA we use certain foreign expressions enough to warrant knowing what they mean. But why this one? I say "oh" often enough, especially since I am always trying to figure things out, but I know when "oh" leaves my lips, it does not fall on the paper as a-u-x and I certainly did not mean "to the", "at the", or "with the". THE AMERICAN

HERITAGE DICTIONARY includes "aux" as an abbreviation for auxiliary, but abbreviations are not bona fide words.

Another word from Scotland. It means "of all" and the word is **ava**. It is also a beautiful name. If you take that beautiful name and say it backwards, you have the next word.

**Ave** does not have a silent "e". Instead, the last letter sounds like a long "a". In the Catholic church, Ave is the saying of the Ave Maria prayer.

Another Scottish entry is **awa** and it means away.

"Great wonder, a feeling of wonder and reverence inspired by anything of great beauty, sublimity, majesty, or power." What an awesome definition for **awe**. It's on page 141 of THE WORLD BOOK DICTIONARY.

A sharp pointed tool, called an **awl**, is used to make small holes in leather or wood.

Then there is the case with ax and **axe**. Why the ax can't be brought down on that silent "e" and save a lot ink, especially when so many copies of The Wizard of Oz are being pumped out, is a question that no one cares to answer.

It means yes. It means affirmative. But your parents and I and Captain Kirk know that it means so much more. It means we have full engine power and it comes from Scotty of Scotland. **Aye.**

Our last word for this letter is **azo**. It's a doozy. THE WORLD BOOK DICTIONARY's definition is on page 143. It says "containing the -N:N- group." Huh?

B

Teacher Tangent #5

Does anyone remember the television show *The Black Sheep Squadron*? It starred Robert Conrad and a close friend and bodyguard for Elvis Presley named Red West. Red West wrote a great Christmas song for Elvis. Anyway, the show was originally named ***Baa Baa Black Sheep*** and it's my guess the executives changed the name of the show because it sounded too wimpy. All I know is, when it had "baa baa" in the title, it wasn't canceled. When the name toughened up, it did get canceled. I hope Red West is doing well. By the way, a synonym for **baa** is bleat.

When I was a kid, **bad** meant good. A new movie would come out and it was bad, so we went to see it many times. Does bad still mean good? I haven't heard it in awhile. Such is the life of a square.

Another word that's lost some of its slang appeal is **bag**. It could mean situation or circumstances. Someone would ask you if you wanted to cause some trouble and you, being an upstanding student of good living, could reply with "That's not my bag." This was replaced, I think, with "Homey don't play that."

Interjections are the clowns of English. They make exclaiming feelings a lot more fun than searching for ideas. One of the least used interjections is **bah**. Let's try to use it in place of profanity and quit letting Ebenezer Scrooge have all the fun.

Is there a difference between a bang and a **bam**?

To **ban** something is to not let it in. Romeo was sent out of town for loving Juliet. He was banished. Rightly so because she was engaged. Everyone forgets that! If you want to be a big shot in Shakespeare class, toss out that you know Juliet was engaged and you'll be further along than most of the other students. She was engaged to...you go find out. The only reason I know is because I played the part. Romeo ran a sword through me.

As a kid, *Batman* was one of my favorite television shows. When he was fighting, big words popped onto the screen to emphasize a hit. Sometimes, **bap** was used. It's not a bona fide word though in Scotland, a small loaf of bread is a bap.

There are sixteen definitions for **bar**. The same word appears again as an entry and then one more time. Why not just call that eighteen definitions? Perhaps I should call THE WORLD BOOK DICTIONARY folks and ask. Alas, I am writing this over the weekend and I'm guessing they are closed. If you are reading this during the work week, give them a call! Ask!

Another meaning for **bat** is to move the eyelashes quickly.

**Bay** is entered six times and the total number of definitions is eighteen. No, I don't know why. It's still the weekend.

If **Bea** Arthur married Bobby Vee, then divorced him and married Rick Dees, she'd be Bea Vee Dees.

There are many definitions for **bed**. The new one for me being that it's the flesh surrounding the base of a claw of an animal.

Don't panic. There's a **bee** in the room. Did you know there are more than twenty thousand species of bees? May they not all come looking for their pal.

We're not supposed to **beg** but no one ever tells us why we shouldn't. Having begged before, I can tell you that there is a bad feeling left in the body after begging because it hurts to want something so badly and be willing to trade self-worth for it. It can extra painful, even dangerous, if it becomes a habit.

Ready for some physics? Don't worry, there is no test at the end of the book. A unit for measuring the differences in the intensity of sound levels is a **bel**. If we capitalize the first letter, then we're talking about the Babylonian god of creation.

Sandra **Bem** is an expert on how our culture views gender.

**Ben** is a great friend. It is also a movie about a rat from the 70's.

In Europe, there is a band called **beo**.

**Bes** was a god in ancient Egypt who entertained newborns.

Pete Rose **bet** on baseball. That, and how he's handled the fallout from it, is keeping him out of the Hall of Fame.

A leader in Turkey can sometimes be called a **bey**. It is pronounced like the word "bay".

If you're eating and wearing nice clothing while reading this book, please get a **bib**.

I love **Bic** pens.

Because of ebay, the word **bid** gets more action these days.

When this book becomes a movie, what **big** star do I want to portray me? Yakko Warner.

Teacher Tangent #6

If you have a toddler in your house, keep his or her toys in a clear plastic **bin**. It's easier to look through the clear walls than dumping all the toys out to get to the bottom while searching for a certain toy.

A **bio** is a short history of yourself.

**Bip** Roberts hit .323 for the Reds in 1992.

Three little letters! Our next word, **bis**, is one I've never heard of and yet it has three meanings! It means twice. In music, it is a direction on the paper to repeat a phrase or passage. It also means encore. Can we yell it at the end of someone's performance? Na.

Remember this **bit**? Two bits, four bits, six bits, a dollar? A bit is twelve and a half cents. Two bits is a quarter. Hold on! Inside this paragraph, there are three meanings for bit. If you think a little bit, you'll come up with the other two.

More slang! Of course, **biz** is short for business but it's also the name of a laundry soap.

So far, **Blu** Cantrell's biggest hit is *Breathe*.

I love Robert **Bly**. Among other things, he's a poet. I got to hug him once, after a grieving walk through downtown Los Angeles. We both have Norwegian DNA.

A **boa** is a snake that kills its prey by wrapping around it and squeezing tightly. I apologize for the violence but nature is that way sometimes.

To **bob** is to float on the surface of water. A bob is a hair style. It's a slang term in England for a shilling. With a capital B, it is the name of my dad and my older brother. Yes. Bob, wearing a bob, could be bobbing on the ocean while holding a bob. It is conceivable. Can we move along?

More British slang. A **bod** is a fellow. Both dictionaries I am using as references fail to mention it's usage as slang in the United States. If someone exercises a lot and is looking healthy, it can be said that they have a nice bod.

Lieutenant Colonel Eric **Boe** is an astronaut.

THE WORLD BOOK DICTIONARY has a fun definition for **bog**. "It's a piece of soft, wet, spongy ground (that) consists chiefly of decayed or decaying moss." Don't believe me? Look it up on page 223.

Every year in Japan, on July 13th through the 16th, there is a Buddhist festival called a **Bon**.

**Boo**. (Didn't mean to scare you.)

To **bop** someone is to hit them. *Bop* is a great country song by Dan Seals that has to do with dancing instead of hitting.

Bert **Bos** lives in France. He has no idea he is in this book.

The larva of a botfly is calied a **bot**. Perhaps a picture should be inserted here.

The archer shot his **bow** accurately. The crowd applauded and he took a bow.

**Box** is a tough sounding word. I keep trying to get expectant mothers to consider it for a boy's name. No one would mess with a kid named Box.

Oh, **boy**, did you know what you were getting into here? *Boy* is a great dance song by Book Of Love.

Charles Dickens used a pen name. It was **Boz**.

**Bra** is short for brassiere but no one abbreviates it. Perhaps bra began as an abbreviated word but as writers used it, they felt funny, and wanted to quickly end the experience of writing it and they began to skip putting the period at the end. When I was a kid, we used to call them over-the-shoulder-boulder-holders.

Teacher Tangent #7

The next word is **bro.** and that abbreviation is meant to be there. THE WORLD BOOK DICTIONARY says bro. gets a period but bra does not. You and I know that people say "Hey bro" all the time and there is no abbreviation. What gives? This requires action:

Dear WORLD BOOK DICTIONARY,

I am writing because it's still the weekend and I assume your offices are closed. The reason that I would be calling is to discuss certain abbreviation policies. I submit that "bro." does not need a period. Perhaps there can be a new entry for "bro." that does not have a period because there is a slight variation on their meanings. The first one, "bro." with a period seems like a legal term to be used in wills and such. The new and improved "bro" (sans the ".") is a slang version of brother when brother may not be a blood relative but a friend. It could also be used without the "." when speaking to a blood relative brother if that blood relative brother is also a friend but not all blood relative brothers are friends.

Love and Kisses,

Tanner Parsons

Author of Mr. Parsons Presents All the Three-Letter Words.


Could have saved myself a lot of time and trouble if I had checked THE AMERICAN HERITAGE DICTIONARY beforehand. They have both "bro." and "bro".


This is a rare linear moment for definitions! **Bub** has a place in the previous argument about "bro.", "bro", and "bra". "Bub" is a fun word to call a brother or a friend. "Bub" and "bro" are synonyms but "bro." and "bub" are not. You wouldn't say "bub" in your will! "Bra" and "bub" are also not synonyms.

Your bro and your bub can also be called a **bud**.

To **bug** someone is to pester them. Don't bug your buds, otherwise, bub, your bros might not cover for you.

Then you'd be a **bum**.

You'd have to wear your hair in a **bun**.

Walking through the weeds, some stickers got stuck in my socks and they hurt. A **bur** is a fancier word for sticker. This entry is usually spelled b-u-r-r. My friend Jon Mersel loves that there are various ways to spell words.

You're late. Did you miss your **bus**?

There are three big conjunctions. One is "and". Another is "or". The third is **but**.

Did you **buy** this book or check it out at the library?

**Bye.**

C

A **cab** is short for taxicab. Isn't "taxi" short for taxicab?

Synonyms for **cad** are boor and churl. None of these words are flattering.

I have **Cal** Ripken Jr.'s rookie card.

A **cam** is a noncircular wheel mounted on a shaft that changes a perfectly good circular motion into a irregular one. Whoa.

If you have to use the **can**, no need to ask, just go.

I love wearing a baseball **cap**, especially of teams that were around when I was a boy. My favorites are the red Washington Senators hat with a cursive W on it like the one Ted Williams wore when he was their manager and the 1971 Angels hat. It has a lower case "a" and a tilted halo on it.

Anything that moves on wheels can properly be referred to as a **car**.

Does anyone call a man **cat** anymore?

Onomatopoeia! Can you believe that **caw** is listed? Yessiree. It means, of course, the sound of a crow.

**Caz** Novak is a New Zealand artist.

Teacher Tangent #8
Now hold everything. Somebody with too much time on their hands came up with a very silly rule. It must have been made when there were only fifty or so words and the dictionary needed some filler because **cee** is in the dictionary and it means the letter "c". Who is going to spell out the extra two vowels? Bureaucrats!

Cartoons can be created on a **cel**. It is short for celluloid.

In the 60's, the Penguin was Burgess Meredith. In the 70's and 80's, the Penguin was Ron **Cey**.

*The Cha-Cha* is a dance. **Cha**, alone, is not a word.

**Chi** is the twenty-second letter of the Greek alphabet.

The Gas We Pass by Shinta **Cho** is a funny and educative book.

Dr. You-Hua **Chu** is an astronomer.

El **Cid** was an eleventh century Spaniard.

It is pronounced like sis but is spelled c-i-s. Yes, **cis** is a word and has to do with atoms on a plane. Your cis flies for free, I think.

A city dweller in archaic times (they had cities in archaic times?) was called a **cit**. I am unsure of who did the name calling but a fight broke out afterwards.

Here is a perfect example of why this book should be by your side at all times. You will probably be the first one to know that a **clo** is a unit for measuring the warmth of a jacket or any garment. THE AMERICAN HERITAGE DICTIONARY has no such entry.

A male swan is called a **cob**.

A **cod** is a fish. Cape Cod is a place. I am sure there must be a limerick about the cad from Cape Cod. If you don't find one after hours of research, feel free to write your own.

David Allan **Coe** wrote the perfect country song.

THE WORLD BOOK DICTIONARY says a lot about **cog**. It can be a mistake, a small boat, or even, according to THE AMERICAN HERITAGE DICTIONARY, a verb having to with cheating during a game of dice. It gets nutty in a sentence about a man who makes a mistake on a small boat while cheating at dice.

The intersection between a trough and a wedge is a **col**.

I just learned that **con** can also mean to learn something well enough to retain the information. Then I counted. There are twenty-four pages of words in THE WORLD BOOK DICTIONARY that begin with "con". Twenty-four pages!

Teacher Tangent #3 squared
From eight grade to eleventh grade, I went to school at the American Community School of Athens, Greece. There was a big Greek boy in some of my classes and his name was Con Theodoropolous. To this day, I love saying his name. It's a poem all by itself.

The sweet sound of a dove is a **coo**.

Did you know that **cop** can also mean to capture?

How about **cor**? It is a British interjection and it is a musical term having to do with an instrument called a mellophone. THE AMERICAN HERITAGE DICTIONARY bypasses this one.

I did well at Geography but flunked Trigonometry. Twice. But I do remember **cos** is short for cosine. It's an abbreviation with no period. Romaine lettuce was introduced on the Greek island of Cos.

I love this one! THE AMERICAN HERITAGE DICTIONARY outdoes itself with **cot**: "People might assume that there is nothing particularly exotic about the history of the word cot. However, *cot* is a good example of how some words borrowed from other cultures become so firmly naturalized over time that they lose their émigré flavor. The British first encountered the object denoted by *cot*, a light frame strung with tapes or rope, in India, where their trading stations had been established as early as 1612. The word *cot*, first recorded in English in 1634, comes from kh , the Hindi name for the contrivance. During subsequent years, *cot* has been used to denote other types of beds, including in British usage a crib."[1]

Another definition for **cow** is to make afraid.

A person who steers a boat and shouts directions to the crew is a coxswain. **Cox** is informal for coxswain. Wally Cox was the voice of Underdog. What do you mean, "Who's Underdog?"

To act more shy than you really are is to be **coy**.

THE WORLD BOOK DICTIONARY says that **coz** is pronounced "kuz". It is the informal word for cousin. Well, if it's informal, why not keep the "kuz"? Why get fancy? The ess becomes zee but the cee cannot become "k"? Down the road we will discover that the informal for "because", which you and I know is "cuz", is NOT listed. Now, I have been to a few formals in my life and none of my cousins were ever there. Why not? Cuz.

If you are a financial wizard, you know that **cru** has something to do with the world's currency. I know very little about money except how to earn, spend, lose, invest, lose some more, fritter away the rest, and never accrue too much of it.

It's okay to **cry**. Next time you find yourself crying, consider how long you can go instead of trying to stop. When you're done, you'll feel like an aquarium that's been thoroughly cleaned.

A baby bear is a **cub** but so is a baby fox, lion, tiger, and many other wild animals. Ernie Banks is Mr. Cub.

The cow eats. The food goes into her first stomach. She barfs it back up. She then chews this slightly digested barf before it heads down to her second stomach. The slightly digested barf is called a **cud**.

---

from THE AMERICAN HERITAGE DICTIONARY OF THE ENGLISH LANGUAGE, FOURTH EDITION.

A stick used to poke the balls on a billiard table is called a **cue**. I used "billiard" instead of "pool" because "pool" might make you think of swimming and it is quite difficult to get a good shot while the white cue ball is sinking rapidly.

In public education, a folder is created for each student and it follows them throughout their education. The folder is called a cumulative folder. Papers are constantly added to it. Educators have shortened "cumulative folders" to "cums", rhymes with "rooms". Your individual folder, bulging with bureaucratic insights about you, can be called a **cum**. Rhymes with "doom". When you graduate from high school, I believe you are allowed to take possession of it. By the way, my two reference dictionaries have more meanings for this one. It is a bona fide word.

Can a **cup** be made of glass? Isn't that just a glass?

A worthless dog of mixed breed is a **cur**. It's still worthy of love.

This letter went well! Let's pretend we're in the movie business on the next one, our final entry for cee.

**Cut!**

D

Teacher Tangent #2+2+2+2+2

When I was a kid, there was a commercial that suggested a **dab** is enough. Nowadays, it feels like they want us to use lots and lots in order that we'll run out and buy more. Lather, rinse, repeat. Use a generous amount. Well, a dab is small. My mother uses that word a lot. She does not want to run out of things and have to make another trip to the store. Conserve. A dab will do.

Teacher Tangent #99 divided by nine.

I love my **dad**. There have been many times I haven't acted that way and went out of my way to show I didn't love him. I felt like I had to break away from him, had to go out on my own and fight the world on my own terms. My life is very good these days and I am grateful that my dad and I have not only healed our relationship, but we get along very well. When my first book came out, he was my number one supporter. He bought a lot of copies and sent them to friends. Many people get lousy dads or never know their dad. I am deeply thrilled that I have had a long and complex relationship with mine. It's made me a better person.

A **dag** is a heavy pistol from long ago and is no longer used. It is also a word the British use for a loose hanging thread.

**Dah** is used in describing the details of Morse Code. Morse Code is made up of dits and dahs.

**Dai** is not in the dictionary but it is the last name of one of the very best students I ever had. She would go into the Mr. Parsons' Students Hall of Fame on the first ballot. Whatever assignment was given, she always went way beyond the expectations.

I'm not sure how to use it in a sentence but a **dak** has to do with transporting mail in India.

In the East Indies, **dal** is a plant. The pea from this plant makes a split pea porridge. It's also the name for another cooked dish made with lentils and spices.

Admirers of profanity love to laugh at this one. **Dam**. It's always fun to watch students trying not to giggle during Science when teaching effective ways to turn a river into a powerful energy source by manipulating the flow of water. If you are new at this game, the curse word sounds the same but adds an en. That makes it a four-letter word and not available as an entry here.

Steely **Dan** was a great seventies band that had a wonderful comeback in the year 2000 with their CD, *Two Against Nature*.

Remember "da", the sword with the black handle that gets swung about in Burma? "Dah" and **dao** are acceptable alternatives to "da". THE AMERICAN HERITAGE DICTIONARY did not let this sword get through the metal detector.

Let's go fishing! When you are letting the bait dip and bop lightly on the water, that's called dapping. **Dap** is a verb that also means to bounce or skip.

Dip, dot, dit, dah, and daw are bona fide words but **dat** is not. What's up with dat?

In North Africa and Europe, there is a small crow called a jackdaw that is often called **daw**.

**Dax** is the name of a Starfleet Lieutenant on *Star Trek: Deep Space Nine*.

A great song to start your **day**? *It's A Beautiful Day* by U2.

A teenage girl from wealthy parents who begins being seen on the town is sometimes referred to as a debutante. Short for debutante is **deb**. I'm not sure if calling someone a deb is appropriate. Is it unkind? My friend Debby in Arizona likes to be called Deb. But that's different. Isn't it?

The letter D is spelled d-e-e. A **dee** is also a cylinder in which electrons fly around in at a rate of up to 28,000 miles per second. No, I can't imagine that speed either.

The 1987 version of THE WORLD BOOK DICTIONARY does not have **def** in it but THE AMERICAN HERITAGE DICTIONARY does include this new slang word. It means excellent. There was a popular rock band in the eighties called Def Leppard. A hairdresser I knew thought their name was Dead Flipper.

My brother Dusty loves the music of **Del** Amitri.

**Dem** Bones is a way of referring to our skeletons. It is also a song. Dem is not a bona fide word.

A good synonym for **den** is lair.

The morning **dew** is a strong image of renewal.

How ironic these two are out of order. In Persian mythology, a **dev** is another way to spell **div**, which means a demon or evil genius. THE AMERICAN HERITAGE DICTIONARY excludes these guys. Must've had a spat. Now, get back in line.

Ever ride in a hot air balloon? I **did**.

Everyone will **die**. But not everyone lives fully. You could.

A few years ago, **dig** was slang for understand. You dig?

Better know what **dim** means in case you're asked. Not knowing may give away the answer.

Annoyingly loud background noise is **din**.

I've always liked Alice Cooper but never got into **Dio**.

Is there anything better than chips and **dip**?

A word that's been created recently! When I was a kid, **dis** was not a word. THE WORLD BOOK DICTIONARY, from 1987, does not include it but THE AMERICAN HERITAGE DICTIONARY, from this century, does. It's short for "disrespect".

This one is going the other direction. As Morse Code becomes obsolete, **dit** will disappear. It's bona fide now. Use it while you can!

Pinochle is a card game. There is a certain play you can make for ten points and it's called a **dix**. Rhymes with "breeze". THE AMERICAN HERITAGE DICTIONARY says nothing about this entry. Good thing it's still the weekend or I'd be spending all my time on the phone.

My dad, retired from the Air Force, refers to doctors as **Doc**. He tells me that every Marine unit has a Navy corpsman, an enlisted man who is not a doctor, who is assigned to tend to wounded Marines. The corpsman is always called Doc. It is a bona fide word.

It's not just a female deer! A **doe** can be the female for almost any animal whose male equivalent is called a buck. The plural of doe? Does. Are you sure you pronounced it correctly?

Sometimes the language of THE WORLD BOOK DICTIONARY is perfect. The first definition of a **dog** is a "four-legged flesh-eating mammal used as a pet, for hunting, and for guarding property." It goes on but I love that intro. Sounds like an exciting new adventure show on NBC that'll be canceled after two episodes.

Homer Simpson has blurted **d'oh** for so many years, dictionaries are going to have to include it in upcoming editions.

A unit to measure pain is a **dol** and is read on a dolorimeter.

Pronounced with a long "o", dom means doum palm. I have no idea what that means but I do remember that Joe DiMaggio had two brothers that played in the major leagues. One was Vince and the other was Dom. In Portugal and Brazil, "Dom" was used as a title, kind of like "Mister". The Scrabble and Boggle players aren't going to let you get away with this one, though.

Sometimes my students and I would be singing *Deck The Halls* before Christmas, er, I mean Winter Break. They did not understand the phrase, "**don** we now our gay apparel." In this sentence, "apparel" means "clothing", "gay" means "happy", and "don" means "to wear". The phrase encourages us to put on our happy clothes. It is also proper to use "don" when referring to a Spanish gentleman. The head of the Mafia can be a don.

Teacher Tangent #12

How can they leave **doo** out of the dictionary? It means poop. It's pronounced exactly like "do". It's short for doo-doo. I guess doo-doo could be plural and doo could be one dropping. Not putting a picture is understandable but to omit it is to have denied the voices of millions of toddlers. Wait. Maybe I'm thinking of poo. Poo and doo are synonyms aren't they? And what about cock-a-doodle-doo?

To steady a diamond while it is being cut, the expensive rock is put into a **dop**. A dop is also the name of a brandy made from grape skins.

A European dung beetle is called a **dor**. Dung beetle sounds more gross and is more fun to say. If you use dung beetle in a sentence, you know someone younger than you is going to ask what a dung beetle is and you get to have all the fun of explaining while watching their face squinch up when they realize dors eat doo-doo. THE AMERICAN HERITAGE DICTIONARY only accepts dor as part of the word "dorbeetle".

It can mean a lot of things but dot with a capital dee is **Dot** and she is soooooooo cute on *Animaniacs*.

A synonym for thrive is the Scottish word **dow**. Our back-up reference, as with a majority of the Scottish words mentioned in this book, does not recognize dow as its own word. But wait, you claim to hear it all the time. The Dow is up or the Dow crashed. That's an informal noun that is short for "The Dow-Jones Industrial Average". Charles Dow was a man who published financial remarks in the late nineteenth century.

There is a rapper named Dr. **Dre**. The vowel is pronounced as a long "a".

I am so not with it! Who is **Dru** Hill? Are they like Jethro Tull? Jethro Tull was a band but many thought it was one guy.

When I was a kid, we sang "How **dry** I am, how wet I'll be, if I don't find the bathroom key." There is another verse about failing to find the key and its consequences but it eludes me.

To **dub** someone is to give them a title. In the entertainment business, it means to add music or other sounds to the picture.

The French word for duke is **duc**. Our American reference does not include this one.

A **dud** is something that fails. If this book doesn't sell well, it will be considered a dud. To keep that from happening, please encourage your friends and family to buy their own copy and quit borrowing yours.

There are several definitions for **due**. If you checked this book out from the library please return it by the due date so someone else can borrow it. A library is a public refuge that keeps you out of the rain while you tour the universe.

The past tense and the past participle of dig is **dug**. If you are extremely juvenile and insist on looking up words having to do with anatomy, you've found a winner with "dug". Look it up in a good thick dictionary and giggle quietly.

"No kidding" is sometimes replaced with "Well, **duh**." Our main reference omits it but our secondary one includes it. Normally, it's the other way around.

The Italian plural of "duo" is **dui**. It works in Italy but not in the USA. Yet, "duo", which is coming up shortly, is a bona fide word in English. Wait a second. Plural? "Duo" means "two" and "two" is already plural. This is a mess and I am simply going to change the subject. With all caps, DUI means "driving under the influence" of alcohol or drugs. It's truly one of the worst things a person can do. Never get in a car with a driver who's had two or more drinks in the last hour.

How often do you see the word **dun**? Hardly ever I bet. Yet, it has several definitions. It needs a press agent. Did you know dun is a color?

Batman and Robin are the Dynamic **Duo**.

An archaic word for opening something is **dup**. Shakespeare used it.

Are you a **dux**? That's the word for the number one student in a class in Scotland.

To **dye** something is to change its color.

I am having a deja vu. There is an animal that is the result of crossbreeding between the domesticated yak and the water buffalo. It's called a **dzo**. I am not making this up. What's crossbreeding? Ask your parents.

E

In archaic Old English, **ean** means to yean and yean means "to bring forth" and both have something to do with pregnant goats. It has nothing to do with crossbreeding. No animals were hurt during the making of this book.

A wise old lady teacher whispered into my **ear** during my subbing years, "They learn in spite of us."

**Eat**. It seems we do. The U.S. Surgeon General (America's Doctor) says more than half of us in the USA are too fat. On the other hand, according to an article on 11/25/2003 at news24.com, 850 million people in our world go to bed hungry. Something must change.

The French word for water is **eau**. The whole thing is pronounced as a long "o". Why not just use the "o"? Yes, the extraterrestrial in the third row...that's a good idea. For those who didn't hear her, she said perhaps it would be mistaken for a zero. THE AMERICAN HERITAGE DICTIONARY remains dry on this one.

To **ebb** can mean to flow. Roy Hamilton sang a great song called *Ebb Tide*. If you are falling in love tonight, play that and it may enhance the swirl of emotions.

Umberto **Eco** is a successful Italian writer.

A letter of the Old English alphabet that got left behind is **edh**. It's sort of our "th" sound. It looked like a capital D with a short line across the middle of the tall straight line.

In West Africa, mainly in southern Nigeria, there is a farming community. A person belonging to this group is called an **Edo** and it also a name for their language.

More than one Ed is **Eds**.

**Edy** Pickens is an artist and teacher in West Los Angeles.


Did you notice the **eel** swimming on our cover? Eels can live in salt or fresh water. I always thought someone should make a comic book hero out of an electric eel, but no one I spoke with could get around the problem of the cape getting soggy.


Teacher Tangent #13

Nuttiness. Absolute lunacy. Apostrophes are suppose to help the writers and speakers by making less work. If I have the words "do" and "not" and I slam them together, I lose a letter in the crunch and save some space with "don't". But this entry defies the logic of apostrophes. It is **e'en**, which is an adverb and means even. The apostrophe helps us lose a letter but the apostrophe itself takes the lost letter's space. Saying "e'en" and trying to make two syllables out of it is much more time consuming than just saying "even", so what's the point? English is a nutty language.


This entry is **e'er**. Same problem.


Fluffy has three **efs** in it.


A small newt is called an **eft**. If you want to bug the teacher, when he or she asks if there are any questions, raise your hand and say, "What's a newt?". If there is uproarious laughter, good job! Suffer

64

your consequences graciously. If there is no laughter, I don't know who you are and you never read this book.

An **egg** is both its shape and its contents.

Elton John has a good song called **Ego**.

A synonym for **eke** is barely.

How come the plural for dwarf is dwarfs but the plural for **elf** is elves? Has there e'er been an elf who was a dwarf?

Will **Eli** Manning surpass his brother? Time will tell.

An **elk** is somehow related to the moose. The plural of moose is moose. The plural of elk is elk. But THE WORLD BOOK DICTIONARY says that "elks" is also acceptable. Do the mooses and elkses ever ponder this controversy whenever two or more of them are gathered?

E'er measured a piece of cloth? That measurement is called an **ell**. Also, one way to spell the letter L is e-l-l. The other way has only one ell.

There are eighteen species of **elm** trees.

Lollipop has three **els**.

In a certain dialect of Old English, **eme** (pronounced with a long e and the final silent e) means an uncle.

**Emo** Phillips says wonderfully silly things. And gets paid to do so!

Mommy has three **ems**.

An **emu** cannot walk backwards.

Na **Eng** works in television production.

I highly recommend *Music For Airports* by Brian **Eno**.

Nunnery has three **ens**.

**Eny** Pavoncello lives in Jerusalem. She makes and sells bibs.

Split **Enz** was an eighties band.

Whoe'er planned the English language should have made the word **end** start with a zee and have it be the last word in the dictionary.

But, the development of English started with a bunch of talkers and, much later, it moved into committees.

Well, which is it? An **eon** is used to describe many thousands of years and can also specifically be used for a billion years.

The Greek Goddess of dawn is **Eos**. After the Romans conquered Greece, Eos got a new name. It was Aurora.

To be clever, capable, and able is to be **ept**.

A period of time is an **era**. It can be a short time or filled with eons.

Teacher Tangent #14

This list, I mean, book, does not include abbreviations. But ERA is a favorite and it gets special inclusion. In baseball, a pitcher tries to keep the hitting team from scoring. Doesn't always happen. When a pitcher gives up a run, and if nobody else on his team made an error, it means the pitcher earned the run. If his teammates erred and the runs scored, the pitcher didn't earn the run. A formula was created that shows the average amount of earned runs a pitcher gives up for a whole game, which is nine innings long. It works like this: Add all the earned runs the pitcher has given up. Take that total and divide it by nine (the innings of an entire game). Since it probably won't go in evenly, use a couple of decimal places. The quotient (and all my students remember what the quotient is) states the pitcher's earned run average. The lowest ERA posted by a starting pitcher in the last eighty-five years is 1.12. The man was Bob Gibson and he was the ace of the St. Louis Cardinals during the 60's.

An archaic word meaning "before" is **ere**.

When someone joins the Royal Air Force in England, they may start at the lowest rank which is an aircraftsman. The nickname for an aircraftsman is **erk**. The word works in England but THE AMERICAN HERITAGE DICTIONARY excludes it.

There is an eagle in Europe with a white tail who usually lives near the sea. It is called an **ern**. It's also okey-dokey to add a silent "e". My friend Jon Mersel loves it when there are multiple ways to spell a word. Didn't I already say that?

To be incorrect is to **err**.

Sassafras begins with an **ess** and has a total of four esses.

Teacher Tangent #15
Take some harsh exercises, a little Zen Buddhism, and some folks who pay a lot of money to become self-realized and you have **est**. Initially "est" stood for Erhard Seminar Training, so it seems like it would

qualify as an acronym. But THE WORLD BOOK DICTIONARY does not use capitals for it and there are no periods in or after the entry so "est" becomes its own word. It is a true acronym in that it holds up as a word without merely pronouncing capitalized initials like, for instance, NBC. "Est" is not an entry in THE AMERICAN HERITAGE DICTIONARY and it did not show up on the top thirty web sites when I entered it on Google. Hmmm....this word came into culture recently. Has it already left?

The upper case seventh letter of the Greek alphabet looks like an English "H". But the lower case of the seventh letter looks more like an en. It is called **eta**, with the vowel being pronounced with a long "a".

Remember "edh"? Well, **eth** is the same thing.

In the summer of '62, Little **Eva** had a number one record with *The Locomotion*. It's still a great song.

The night before the next day can be called the **eve**. On December 23rd, I always mention to at least one person that it's Christmas Eve eve. No one's ever laughed.

I went to high school with a girl named **Evi**. It was short for Evgenia.

A female sheep is a **ewe**. If you capitalize the "e" in "ewe", you get "Ewe". A Ewe is a member of a tribe who lives on both sides of the Togo and Ghana border. Find an atlas.

EXTRA BONUS LESSON!

Perhaps you noticed that in that last sentence, I did not write "an" before "ewe". Why wouldn't I? Raise your hand if you know the answer. Yes, you there wishing we'd go out to P.E., tell me why I didn't write "an" in front of "ewe" when "ewe" begins with a vowel? Correct! Very good. It's because the first letter, despite being a vowel, is pronounced as consonant. Can't fool ewe.

Okay, let's skip **eye** and go to P.E. cuz eye no ewe can't stand this any longer and Eye need a brake.

F

The term **fab** is short for fabulous. The Beatles were often called *The Fab Four*.

A good synonym for **fad** is trendy. Trendy is actually a trendier way to speak of fads. It's not fashionable to use fad.

The British use **fag** as slang for a cigarette. It can also mean to tire from work.

Where's the line between being a **fan** and being a fanatic?

The best visual ever done on the difference between near and **far** was done by Grover of *Sesame Street*. He would run close to the camera for near and then run away to the back of the screen, which made him much smaller, and he'd yell "far". He kept going back and forth to accentuate his point. He got very tired.

If sugar is the new tobacco, is **fat** the new lung cancer?

Teacher Tangent #16

A facsimile is an exact copy. As a kid collecting baseball cards, I liked when Topps put facsimile autographs on the cards. That's how I learned about this word. I thought it meant fake. The player signed his name once and Topps reproduced it many times on the cards. It's much easier than to fanatically hunt the guy down and get him to sign it. But sometimes I did that. In 1971, I was ten years old and I had Oscar Gamble's rookie card. He was playing for Eugene, the Phillies farm team. I walked up to him as he sat in the dugout, I don't know how I got on the field but he was beaming! He had never seen his own card before and he not only signed it, he showed it to his teammates, and had a long talk with me. I still have that card, with his real autograph over the facsimile one. Oh, wait. "Facsimile" is, let me count them, a nine letter word. Nine letter words are not explored for several more volumes. Why the big deal? The word **fax** is short for facsimile.

Teacher Tangent #Four squared plus one.

The definition of **fay** is **fey**. So helpful. Flipping slightly ahead to page 789 in our main reference, fey carries a lot of weight in all its meanings. It can mean lively. It can mean elfin. It can mean crazy. It can mean a behavior suggesting there will be sudden doom. The best one is that it can mean to be a visionary. Consider being a visionary when you grow up. We used to have lots of them. Dr. Martin Luther King Jr. was one. We need more. It does not pay well.

Offer food to an FBI agent. Do not assume the Fed's been **fed**.

Ask to have me speak at your graduation. The **fee** is modest.

"Feminine" and "effeminate" can both be shortened to **fem**.

It's a type of Chinese money. It's a wet soggy patch of bog. Toss a **fen** into the fen and make a wish.

Both **fet** and **feu** are in THE WORLD BOOK DICTIONARY but not in THE AMERICAN HERITAGE DICTIONARY. The former is Old English and the latter is Scottish.

If a couple is two than a **few** must be at least three. "Some" is even more vague. If only we would convert to the metric system.

Have you ever seen a round red hat with a black tassel on one side worn by Egyptians and Turks? That nifty hat is called a **fez**. Steely Dan has a song called *The Fez*. It is also the name of a town in Morocco.

When you lie about something that is not a big deal, that's a **fib**.

On sailing ships, there are masts. On the topmast, there is a bar that is square, heavy, and it's there for support. It is called a **fid**. "Fid" can also mean a pile.

It's interjection time! Please welcome the word **fie**! It rhymes with "try", "why", and "high". I often think of interjections as happy things, but this time, it's a bummer. It means "shame". It's from long ago and doesn't get used much anymore. What a fie.

A **fig** is a small, sweet, oblong or pear-shaped fruit that grows in warm regions.

You recognize a **fin** on a shark or dolphin but what about Abraham Lincoln? A five dollar bill is sometimes called a fin.

What are the odds that the next definition would also be about money? I don't know and don't have time to figure them out but **fip**, apparently, is a word. It is short for a fippenny bit which was a coin worth about six cents. Was this in England? Our number two reference has nothing on fips. William Shakespeare never used them. The morale here is, don't except a fip as legal tender.

There is a tree in the pine family called a **fir**.

Both the **fit** and the unfit can throw a fit.

THE WORLD BOOK DICTIONARY uses more than 125 words to define **fix** before it mentions that it means to repair or mend something.

When you pour a soda and hear it bubbling, that's called "fizz". Using only one zee is okay with THE WORLD BOOK DICTIONARY but not THE AMERICAN HERITAGE DICTIONARY. Jon Mersel, a proud American, is okay if you spell it f-i-z. **Fiz** can be a noun or verb.

**Flo** is short for Florence, but it's not in the dictionary.

Influenza is awful. You know it better as the **flu**. Next time you are sick with the flu, use "influenza". It sounds more serious than the flu and could illicit more sympathy. Or perhaps sympathy is not what you are looking for. You can just keep feeling miserable and telling everyone you're fine. How am I supposed to know? This is all so one-sided!

Hythoris Beard, a former student of mine, sang *I Believe I Can* **Fly**. It made me feel like I could.

Do your jeans have a little pocket inside the big pocket? It's called a **fob**. "Fob" can also mean a short watch chain or to trick someone.

Your opponent in any game you play is your **foe**.

Very low clouds that we walk in are called **fog**.

It's interjection time again! Yippee! I'm turning a cartwheel! This interjection is not positive either. It's **foh**. The vowel is long, the last letter is silent, and it means disgust. THE AMERICAN HERITAGE DICTIONARY says nothing of "foh" but William Shakespeare used it in <u>King Lear</u>, <u>Hamlet</u>, and <u>The Merry Wives of Windsor</u>.

In Benin, a country in West Africa, the people and their language there are called **Fon**. It rhymes with Ron and Don instead of won and ton.

I like the song *My Hero* by the **Foo** Fighters.

Are you a guy who is proud of how nicely you dress and strut around? That's what a **fop** does.

**For** is a preposition and a conjunction. Steve Duin graciously wrote the foreword to this book. He points out that Alexandre Dumas, the man who wrote The Three Musketeers, created a famous phrase that ONLY uses three-letter words: *All for one and one for all.*

In Scotland, a drunk can be called a **fou**, which rhymes with "fool" without the ell. It probably came from a drunk who was too inebriated to say the whole word and passed out before getting to the last letter.

How old am I? I remember when there was no **Fox** Television.

An old fashioned word for party is **foy**. Joe Foy of the Red Sox played third base and got two hits in the 1967 World Series.

An adverb meaning to go back is **fro**.

**Fry** can mean a single slice of fried potato, a cooking verb, a small fish or child, to get sun burnt, or to be electrocuted.

To lie or trick someone is to **fub** them. THE AMERICAN HERITAGE DICTIONARY does not include this entry. Or the next one!

A fuddy-duddy is a person from the old school who doesn't like change. **Fud** is short for fuddy-duddy. Fud is also a character in <u>Oh Say Can You Say</u> by Dr. Seuss. Fud has twenty brothers.

A noun and a verb, **fug** has multiple meanings. One has to do with being uncomfortable with stale air in a room.

There are people in Africa, called Fula, who speak **Ful**.

I hope you are having **fun** reading this book.

Ever been sick and have that feeling of paste on your tongue? That gross film can be referred to as **fur**.

G

There are three entries for **gab**, which seems natural. The informal one is most often heard and has to do with talking. I had a student named Gabby and she was aptly named. I could have been named Gabby because I got in trouble for talking more than once. Gabby, however, is much brighter than I was at that age. She may be much brighter than I am at this age.

To **gad** is to wander around. It is also a pointed mining tool.

Another verb and another Scottish entry: **Gae** means to go and also to graze. It is not in THE AMERICAN HERITAGE DICTIONARY.

A joke can sometimes be called a **gag**.

Teacher Tangent #18

Another word for girl is **gal**. My mother used this word a lot when she was younger but one doesn't hear it much any longer. It is informal and it is not, to my knowledge, derogatory. "Gal" is also a unit for measuring the acceleration of gravity. It was named for Galileo. If you are a student who is convinced that you're right about something and can prove it, you'd like Galileo. He found out things nobody knew and after he told the truth about his findings, he was threatened with death. I dare you to learn about what he went through.

A **gam** is a group of whales.

**Gan** is the past tense of gin. Both "gan" and "gin" are archaic words, although "gin" has evolved into other meanings. We'll discuss "gin" in a few paragraphs, but "gan" is gone.

The **Gap** is a clothing store. A gap can be an open space. In baseball, it is the area between fielders in the outfield. I was on a softball team with a bunch of smart alecks. Whenever our hitters knocked a ball through the space between the outfielders, which made the fielders have to turn and run towards the fence, we would shout out, "They're shopping at the Gap!"

Well, it was funny then.

There are garfish. It's okay to call one a **gar**. Gars swim in the rivers of the good ole USA.

Are we all mature here? Let's try. The short term for gasoline is **gas**. There. Did we get through that without snickering?

There's a Hindu form of music called a raga. The final section of a raga is often signified by a **gat**. "Gat" is also a synonym for channel, the wet geographical type, not the TV term.

When the Nazis ran Germany, they divided up the country into political areas called gaus, something like the U.S. is divided into states. The singular would be **gau**.

For a long time, **gay** usually meant happy.

Did you know that the Egyptians used to worship a goddess named Nut? She was married to **Geb**. Many gods and goddesses don't use last names.

In Scotland, a **ged** is a pike. Okay....what's a pike?

Can you believe **gee** has four entries? Be careful when you use it because one of the meanings is telling your ox to turn right.

It's a noun. It's a verb. It's a must for so many who want their hair to be perfect. It's **gel**, which I assumed was short for gelatin but the THE WORLD BOOK DICTIONARY doesn't go there. THE AMERICAN HERITAGE DICTIONARY does! My assumption was correct.

A **gem** is a beautiful rock. The gem business would prefer that we call rocks, "stones", and I'm sure they could justify the distinction but I, for one, will roll my eyes at it.

THE WORLD BOOK DICTIONARY includes it. THE AMERICAN HERITAGE DICTIONARY omits it. The word is **gen** and it is British slang for inside information.

A **Geo** is a car. It's made out of rock.

**Get** is one of the rare words whose pronunciation is exactly like it is spelled.

The Scots bring in another word, this time from page 897 of our main reference. It's pronounced like "gay" but it's spelled g-e-y. It means "considerable". You guessed it, our number two reference does not include it.

Would you like some ghee? It is liquid butter used in India and it comes from boiling and straining milk from buffaloes and cows. It is also appropriate to spell it **ghi**. Smile Jon!

Teacher Tangent #19

**GI's** goes in this book because it has three letters. I don't know if it's ever been used as written text but "GIs" without the apostrophe has been spoken many times as a plural. GI, as noted previously, stands for "government issue". It's another word for soldier. If you have more than one soldier (and you should if you are going to have an army) that makes it plural. THE WORLD BOOK DICTIONARY says the plural is with the apostrophe and I think that would be wrong because the apostrophe suggests ownership. We could write "the GI's gun" or "the GI's letter" but if a bunch of them walk into the casino, I argue that a bunch of "GIs" just came in. A hush would settle in the room, not because of the people inside were trying to think of whether or not to use the apostrophe but because, in many war movies, when the GIs come in, mirrors start breaking, bullets start flying, everyone has to duck for cover.

Note to self: Remember to delete the previous paragraph. Or at least rewrite it or talk to a General about it first. Check facts concerning GIs walking into casinos in war movies. Remember to floss.

You think that was bad. **GI'd** is a verb.

Male cats will tell you of a very painful definition for **gib**.

"Gic" is not a word but **gid** is. Go figure. Actually, stay and learn, because the morbid among us may like the definition. "Gid" is a noun having to do with baby tapeworms inside the brain of a sheep which makes the sheep less smarter than usual. As a teacher, I refrain from using the term "dumb" but I recall the expression "dumb as sheep". Well, if a sheep has gone gid and is actually dumber than regular sheep, what phrase should we use?

The Scottish use **gie** (pronounced gee) to mean to give. I hope this book sells well in Scotland.

A job is a **gig**. It's mostly associated with musicians getting a paying job. Musicians love gigs. Especially **Gil**. Gil Sanchez is an excellent guitar player from Albuquerque.

My dad likes to drink **gin** on the rocks.

A short noun for gypsy is **gip**.

Get is sometimes spoken with an accent and then transferred to texts as **git**. It doesn't happen very often.

A **gnu** is an African antelope. There are different kinds of gnus. Who knew?

In Tibet, there is a gazelle with a black tail and it's called a **goa**.

A whole bunch of something can be called a **gob**. It is also a nickname for a sailor in the United States Navy. I'm guessing that both meanings are becoming archaic.

Teacher Tangent #20

Ut-oh. How can I discuss **God** without starting trouble? The events of the day are showing once again the clash between differing views of God. Differing views of God even break up families. Oh, how I wish that "God" had more than three letters! Especially since part of the task in this book is to define things and if I could define God, then I not only would have a best seller, but I'd probably get my own talk show, too. If I got my own talk show, my guests would be stars I liked as a kid and it would be canceled soon enough because the younger generation would not recognize the cast of *Land of the Giants* or *Time Tunnel*. Nor would they recognize my co-host Nolan Ryan since he hasn't struck anyone out in more than a decade. And my band leader, Alice Cooper, hasn't had a top ten single since 1989. But he's made great tunes in this new century, like *Clowns Will Eat Me* and we'd play it every night which is another reason we'd get canceled quickly. Back to the matter at hand. I'm trying to avoid trouble, which is a sure way to keep sales of the book low. I could skip God with a capital G and just mention the word "god". A good synonym for god is deity. Whew. Hope god with a capital G is okay with how i handled this one.

Out of the frying pan and into the fire...the next word is **Gog**, which is a place and a person. It's a prince in the book of Ezekiel in the Old Testament and it's a nation in the New Testament that joins in fighting against the kingdom of God during the battle of Armageddon which some people believe has to do with the end of the world.

Thick sticky stuff that's hard to wash off is **goo**.

The past tense and past participle of get is **got**.

Jewish people use **goy** to describe someone who is not Jewish. Sometimes it is used to describe a Jewish person who is not practicing Jewish traditions. Sometimes it is derogatory, sometimes it's not. Be careful.

In <u>One Fish Two Fish Red Fish Blue Fish</u> by Dr. Seuss, a boy gets to box a **Gox**.

Teacher Tangent #21

It's difficult to ask children to get rid of their **gum** because I enjoy gum. I feel like a hypocrite but one reason behind not allowing gum at school is that many children do not spit their gum into the trash and imagine allowing hundreds of kids to chew gum! What if just a few fail to put it into the trash? I never met anyone who likes taking gum off their shoes and that's the main rationale behind not allowing it.

When you want to focus on a goal and try your very best, it can be said that you will **gun** for it.

A coarse sugar of southeastern Asia is called **gur**. When the "g" is capitalized to make "Gur", we're talking about a large group of West African languages. THE AMERICAN HERITAGE DICTIONARY has nothing for "gur".

**Gus** Gil played shortstop for the Seattle Pilots. The Pilots were a Major League Baseball team for only one year. It was 1969.

Inside the middle of your body is sometimes called a **gut**.

It is British slang to call the governor, **guv**.

Teacher Tangent #22

**Guy** Papageorge was my neighbor in Athens, Greece. We played football together. He was the best player on our bad team. I may have been the worst player. During our only victory, I broke through the line and sacked quarterback Donald Sherman all by myself. As happy as I was to finally do something right and help our team; Guy Papageorge nearly lost his mind expressing his exuberance to me. He was shouting and pounding my back. He was very happy I'd figured out how to play football.

Gymnasium is such a great sounding word. The mouth really fluctuates when saying gymnasium, like it does when saying the name of my old classmate, Con Theodoropolous. It's a shame that gymnasium is constantly shortened into **gym**.

"I've been gypped!" is a cry from someone who feels cheated on a deal. The root is **gyp** but it's wrong to use it because it is short for gypsy. It is worse than being impolite. There are still gypsies in this world and it's rude to put other people down. Instead, yell out that you've been swindled. Wait. Swindlers may be offended. The very best thing is for all of us to check our transactions carefully and not allow ourselves to be cheated.

Whew, this letter's been stressful.

H

The past tense and past participle of have is **had**. Yes, a nice easy start.

The Scottish sometimes use **hae** in place of have. Now, all this time I have been putting in the Scottish entries only to have THE AMERICAN HERITAGE DICTIONARY deny most of them and leaving me without dual support from my references. Until now.

My second reference dictionary calls it a "transitive verb". Hip hip hooray!

A very ugly old woman can be referred to as a **hag**. I suggest you not be the one doing the referring.

Ha! Interjection time! Ha can also be written as **hah**. So there.

Pronounced like hi, the Japanese word for yes is **hai**.

When a Muslim makes a pilgrimage to Mecca, it is called a hajj or a **haj** or even a hadj.

Do not name your computer **Hal**.

When you're eating **ham**, know that it's the upper part of a hog's hind leg.

**Han** is the first name of a great character in *Star Wars* and it is also the name of dynasty in China that lasted for over four hundred years.

**Hao** Asakura is an evil anime character.

Another word for luck is **hap**.

The definition of **has** is a doozy. It is the third person singular present indicative of "have". Memorize it, use it at parties, and people will no longer invite you.

I love a good **hat**.

There are several entrees for **haw**. One is a command shouted to an ox to turn left.

Grass, alfalfa, or clover that's been cut and dried so animals can eat it is called **hay**.

*Hee Haw* was a television show. 'Haw' is a word. **Hee** ain't. But what about when writers write "hee hee" to denote laughter? Huh?

Hugh Hefner's nickname is **Hef**.

In Norse mythology, the goddess of death was named **Hel**. Her dad was Loki. I don't know if he was proud of her or not.

Look at your shirt or pant leg bottom. See where the edge has been carefully sewn? That's called a **hem**. It's on the border of almost all clothing.

A female bird is often referred to as a **hen**.

The word "cool" doesn't seem to ever go out of style. Hip is nearly as strong as cool. Both dictionaries note that **hep** can be used for hip but why bother when hip sounds so cool? Fashion has gotten to the point where being unhip is cool. And vice-versa.

*Have You Seen **Her*** by the Chi-Lites is a great 70's song.

I was in a Men's Group for more than ten years. I am still an honorary member. One of the things we did was sing *For **He's** A Jolly Good Fellow* whenever someone in the group did a worthy feat. It looks corny on paper but it sounds great both in the boisterous singing of it and on the smiling side of receiving it.

Wow! **Het** is a word and it's not even archaic! I can't recall ever reading or hearing it. It is the past tense and past participle of "heat". THE AMERICAN HERITAGE DICTIONARY skips it.

A serious word for cutting is **hew**. We're not talking scissors here. One can hew their way through the forest with an ax or other big blade.

A spell induced from witchcraft is called a **hex**.

**Hey**, when you're hewing away the forest, make sure it's not a rain forest.

The sound of a hiccup is called a **hic**.

Teacher Tangent #23

I had the hiccups for more than a week. It was painful and beyond annoying. I could not sleep despite trying every strange method of making them disappear. How did I finally over come them? I was on second base and someone singled to the outfield. I tore around third and knew the play at home was going to be close. I slid head first. The banging of my chest to the ground as I crossed home plate knocked them out of me. I jumped up and ran to the dugout in disbelief that they were gone. My teammates gave me high fives. Their jubilance had nothing to do with my cure. They were happy I'd been safe.

My wife loves to tell the story of being a little girl and playing hide and seek with her family. She won the game after she quietly **hid** in the bathtub. She is still proud of that one.

Vikki Carr's biggest hit was *It Must Be **Him***.

A Hebrew unit of liquid measurement is called a **hin**. One hin is a slightly more than one gallon.

**Hip** has many definitions. The one I am learning as I write is that hip is the seedcase holding the ripe seed of a rosebush.

I think **his** would be more interesting if it was spelled the way it's pronounced, which is h-i-z.

I know a principal who does not step in at the beginning of a fight. She steps in after some punches are thrown. She wants to let the brawlers feel how terrible it is to be **hit** in such a manner. She believes experience is the better teacher.

Fireplaces used to be a place to cook meals. Set on the back wall of such fireplaces was a shelf to keep food warm. The shelf was called a **hob**.

Ever seen a **hod**? It's a tool with a long straight handle that has a trough on one end in order for a worker to carry cement or bricks on their shoulder.

Another tool is a **hoe**. It also has a long thin handle but on the end is a thin blade used to remove weeds and turn the soil.

A **hog** is a pig weighing over a hundred twenty pounds. Quite often, though, "hog" and "pig" are used interchangeably. Hog is also a basketball game that is played when there's no time for horse. Or is that Pig?

My wife and I never call each other dear but often use **hon**, even though it's not a bona fide word. Our love could care less.

Teacher Tangent #24

As we traipse through the land of three letter words we come across yet another interjection. It's happening so often that it feels correct to create theme music for whenever an interjection appears. When you see "Interjection Time!" have some trumpets trumpeting or some drums thumping. Please provide your own. You can wait for the next interjection because I know I didn't give much lead time into this paragraph. Whatever music is playing is sufficient for now. If it's quiet, then hum as we learn about **hoo**. It means excitement and/or delight. It goes really well with "woo". Homer Simpson often says "woo-hoo". Someone who wants your attention might use "yoo-hoo". THE AMERICAN HERITAGE DICTIONARY mentions "yoo-hoo" and even "hoo-ha" but not "hoo" all by itself.

**Hop** on Pop is a great Dr. Seuss book.

*It's **Hot** Tonight* is a great song by Alice Cooper from 1977. It completely captures that late evening misery when you realize the stale heat is going to remain all night long. Those of you with air conditioners have no idea what I'm talking about.

If you want to sound sophisticated, insert "by what means" any time you plan to use the word **how**. Sophistication has not been hip for a long time so be careful. Perhaps you are slick enough to pull it off. By what means? Don't ask me. I am incredibly simple.

**Hoy** is an interjection (cue music) to get someone's attention. It is also a type of small ship that is no longer used.

The central part of a wheel is called the **hub**.

**Hud** Fuddnuddler is one of twenty-one brothers created by Dr. Seuss.

Sometimes **hue** is shouting out a warning, but mostly it's used when someone is getting very picky about a color.

Teacher Tangent #25

Get a **hug**! Dr. Leo Buscaglia believed that everyone should receive five hugs a day. Every day! He's dead now but I'd have voted for him for President. Get your five hugs today. Get them every day.

If there was a Top Forty chart of the most frequently asked questions, I bet "**huh**?" would be in the top five. Teenager Alma Siulagi submits that it is the Number One word among adolescents.

If you were in a club in Hawaii, you'd belong to a **hui**. THE AMERICAN HERITAGE DICTIONARY, disagrees. It claims that "hui" is one of several ways to spell the name of a member of a Muslim people in Northwest China.

A member of the communist guerilla movement in the Philippines is called a **Huk**, which is short for the Talalog (the language of the Philippines) word, Hukbalahap.

I think **hum** should be spelled h-u-m-m because when people say the word, nobody stops at the first em.

A **Hun** was a member of an Asian army that attacked Europe around seventeen hundred years ago. Their leader was named Attila.

If you join the army, you'll have to march. While marching, you'll be counting. Instead of starting at one, you'll start with **hup** or sometimes **hut**. Hup equals one. Hut also equals one. But hup does not equal hut because you can't sleep in a hup.

Another word for depression is **hyp**. THE AMERICAN HER---, yeah, that one, has nothing for "hyp". How depressing.

I

*Painted Ladies* by **Ian** Thomas never gets played on the radio.

In Nigeria, there are a number of people who are Ibos. The first phoneme is a long "e". One of these people is called an **Ibo**.

Paul **Iby** is an Ordained Bishop in Eisenstadt, Austria.

**Ice** is a fun word in the land of music and metaphors. Cold as ice... hot ice...Ice Cube...Icehouse...ice in the veins...ice on fire...you probably know some others. On the other hand, ice is not fun to drive on.

I bet that **ick** is the root word for icky and icky-poo. Oops. Wrong. It's not a word. Can I have my lunch money back?

**Icy** roads are very dangerous.

**Ida** Lupino was an actress who also directed movies. If you want to sound like an artist, say "films" instead of "movies".

In the fresh waters of northern Europe, there is a fish swimming around called an **ide**.

**Idy** is a girl's name.

Teacher Tangent #26

Hey, we're going back to Nigeria! A very long time ago, there was a culture in western Africa that made especially fine bronze sculptures. An adjective to describe this culture is **ife**. It's pronounced with two syllables and both vowels have the long "e" sound. Ife antiques are quite special. Just for fun, I typed in "Ife" on Google's search engine and was taken to a letter discussing an alumni fundraising dinner for a college in Nigeria called the Obafemi Awolowo University. It is called Ife for short. Their college is working hard on fighting sickle cell anemia and needs money. Send a donation.

President Eisenhower's nickname was **Ike**.

People like me are my **ilk**. People like you are your ilk. It has more to do with character than physical characteristics. For example, when I was younger I joked about wanting to be a bum when I grew up. Turns out, bums and I have little in common. They are not my ilk. Hey, saints are not my ilk either. I'm somewhere in between.

So many meanings! Some synonyms for **ill** include...adverse, unkind, sick, defective, inefficient, wicked, and harmful.

**I'll** is an extra efficient contraction in that the apostrophe wipes out two letters.

A small evil spirit is an **imp**.

Are we out of **ink** yet?

When needing rest from travel, sleep at an **inn**. I read that hotels have taken the place of inns. What could possibly be the difference?

I bet **ins** is mostly used when someone is showing you something that is new to you. Erica the librarian will show you the ins and outs of the library she operates. Maybe you know the ins and outs of video games. With video games, I only know the outs.

Atoms sometimes throw their electrons around. Other atoms pick them up, then THEY have too many, and they throw them off to other atoms and havoc occurs, generally followed by mayhem. When an atom has more or less electrons than it normally has, that atom is called an **ion**.

**Ira** is a boy's name.

Someone is angry! Another is mad! A synonym for fury is **ire**.

To annoy someone is to **irk** them. Don't raise the ire of the teacher by irking them.

My mother was born in Iowa from Norwegian parents. She uses a word that means yucky. If I were to pick up a tissue that had a lot of snot in it, she would stop me by yelling, "**Ish**!" If I ran my fingers through dad's ashtray...ish! I'm guessing it's a Norwegian phrase. It's not in either dictionary we're using. My mom got it from her mom. I use it to keep my children from playing in the toilet.

Ladies and Gentlemen! (Don't start the interjection theme music, this is a contraction!) Now presenting the most efficient contraction in the English language. Take "it" and slam it with "would" and get **it'd**. That apostrophe is saving four spaces!

Dr. Kiyosi **Ito** is an award-winning mathematician from Japan.

Possessives use apostrophes. Except this one. **Its** is a possessive without an apostrophe. **It's** is not a possessive. It is a contraction for the words "it is". It is confusing and I trust I have muddled things further. I'd rather talk about Presidents, trains, and baseball.

**I've** only met one President and that was Gerald Ford. We chatted at a Hollywood shindig!

On the make-believe island of Sodor, where Thomas the Tank Engine plays, there is a red engine named **Ivo** Hugh.

On July 4, 1997, I went to Wrigley Field in Chicago with my good friend, Tom Jones (not the singer). It was beach towel day. The **ivy** on the wall is much prettier in person than on television.

On February 19, 1945, the Allies began the invasion of **Iwo** Jima. More than six thousand Americans died during the victory. More than eighteen thousand Japanese defenders died. I learned these details at the U.S. Marine Corps web site.

J

In the boxing arena, a **jab** is a punch. In other places, a jab is to poke with a pointed object. Both hurt.

My parents like the show *JAG*. With a small first letter, **jag** can mean a sharp point, to drink too much, or tear something without care and leave jagged edges.

**Jah** is short for Yahweh which is a name for God in the Old Testament.

**Jal**, New Mexico has a population of about two thousand people.

I was jamming in the car, listening to some jams while eating **jam** when a traffic jam jammed up my jamming.

**Jan** Stenerud, who kicked for 1699 points in the NFL, is in the Pro Football Hall-of-Fame. He was born in Norway.

There are two negative uses for **jap**. Save yourself trouble and just never use it. Ever.

To rock someone out of being stuck is to **jar** them.

A person from Punjab, Sind, or even Northwestern India may be called a **Jat**. It is a friendly term.

**Jaw** can be a metaphor for talking too much. Quit jawing!

**Jay** is mostly associated with birds but it can also pinch hit for stupid, which is a good thing because stupid is so completely impolite that it seems like a curse word now. How jay is that?

**Jeb** Bush lives in Florida.

**Jed** Clampett is a fictitious fellow on *The Beverly Hillbillies.*

Rubert **Jee** runs the Hello-Deli in Manhattan. Perhaps you've seen him on *The Late Show With David Letterman.*

**Jen** is short for "Jenny", which is short for "Jennifer", which is short for "Jenniferbennifer" but the bennifer is silent and rarely written.

Before the middle of the twentieth century, what did **jet** mean? It meant a liquid or gas moving with great force. No jokes please.

A person who practices the religion of Judaism is Jewish. **Jew** is short for Jewish.

**Jez** Alborough wrote <u>Hug</u>. It is twenty-nine pages long but the author only uses three words for the entire story!

A sailing ship may have a triangular sail in the front called a **jib**. There's an inner jib, outer jib, even a flying jib. A jib also is a verb that means to go sideways.

A quick and happy dance is a **jig**. This entry also gets used in the phrase "the jig is up" which means it's over, the end, kaput.

Dr. **Jil** T. Geller is a scientist and an engineer at the Lawrence National Laboratory. Her mother invented her unique name.

Teacher Tangent #27

As a kid, I had a baseball coach who saw how frustrated I was not being a good hitter. He tossed extra batting practice just for me and was always noticing improvement. I improved slightly as a hitter but what amazes me today is that someone cared to help with what must have seemed a fruitless endeavor. Thanks **Jim** Schulteis, wherever you are.

My **job** is to be a good housedaddy and to bang on these keys.

I love my Uncle **Joe**.

To **jog** is not only to run but it is also to push.

John is a name and a bona fide word. **Jon** is just a name.

Michael **Joo** was born in upstate New York and makes his living as a sculptor.

The rhythmic second movement of a typical raga is a **jor**.

To write a short phrase or number down quickly is to **jot**. It looks more strange to the eye than it sounds to the ear because it is spoken more than written.

Can you believe **jow** is in THE WORLD BOOK DICTIONARY? It's a verb to ring a bell for the Scottish. It's not in THE AMERICAN HERITAGE DICTIONARY. It hasn't been used in any English language literature in many decades.

**Joy** is a noun, a verb, a soap, and sometimes a first name.

Binta **Jua** is a gorilla in the Brookfield Zoo in Chicago, Illinois.

**Jud** is one of Fud's and Hud's many brothers in <u>Oh Say Can You Say</u> by Dr. Seuss.

Besides being a container for liquids, **jug** can be a verb to describe the act of birds huddling together.

In North Korea, there is money called a **jun**. A hundred jun is a won. Honest. Would two thousand pounds of jun be jun ton?

In France, gravy is called **jus**. THE WORLD BOOK DICTIONARY gives the pronunciation as (zhy). THE AMERICAN HERITAGE

DICTIONARY includes "au jus", which translates from the French as "with juice" but it does not include "jus" alone.

When being stubborn, a person may raise their head and stick out their chin. To stick out is to **jut**. You ever jut your chin?

K

A Hebrew unit of dry measure is a **kab**. How many kabs fill a cab?

**Kae** Bender is a writer and a yoga instructor in Tennessee.

Whatever happened to **Kai** Foster?

The word Khan has to do with a title of authority and respect in the Eastern Hemisphere. It can also be spelled k-a-n, **kan**, but it loses some oomph. The AMERICAN HERITAGE DICTIONARY does not include "kan". Hey, that reminds me.

Teacher Tangent #28
My favorite movie is *Star Trek II: The Wrath of Khan*. I have the soundtrack but rarely play it because I get so emotional when I relive the attacks of the Enterprise and the death of...oh wait...you're young...you may not know who dies in this movie. Hmmm. Okay. Here's what you do.

1. Watch all 72 episodes of the original series.* Quickly get over your opinion of the quality of the special effects.

2. Skip the first movie, *Star Trek: The Motion Picture*.

3. Watch the next one, *Star Trek: The Wrath of Khan*.

* If time is a consideration...simply watch Episode 24 called *Space Seed*.

In Arabia and Africa, **kat** is a leaf and/or shrub that grows on some trees.

Near the Missouri River, there lived a tribe called Kansa. That is how Kansas got its name. A **Kaw** is a member of that tribe.

In New Zealand there is a large parrot called a **kea**.

Remember Nut? She was the goddess married to Geb. Geb also goes by **Keb**.

This definition doesn't help much. THE WORLD BOOK DICTIONARY says, on page 1147, "**ked** (ked), n. = sheep ked". Well, if I don't know what a ked is, how can I know what a sheep ked is? They must be kedding.

When Christine's little sister began talking, the baby used **Kee** for Christine. Christine liked it so much, she kept it. Christine grew up to be Kee Malesky, the librarian for National Public Radio.

Sometimes after taking medicine, you get drowsy. That's **kef**.

A **keg** is a small barrel that holds less than ten gallons.

Here's a fun word that you can use right away. Besides being Barbie's boyfriend, **ken** is all the things you can see right now. It's your personal viewing screen of the world. Besides these words, what's in your ken right now? "Ken" can also mean the total range of knowledge. Are the times tables in your ken? I have a friend named Ken who married a woman who saved all her Barbies from childhood.

One **key** to success is to live in the present. I did this long ago and plan on doing so in the future but at present, I'm busy.

I don't know anyone who drives a **Kia**.

Teacher Tangent #29

As a teacher, I find that whenever I call a young boy or girl a **kid**, they don't respond favorably. They usually wince or grimace. Generally speaking, a group of children don't mind being called kids but a single child does. It's a reminder that everyone likes to be treated as a person first.

Another word for hemp is **kif**.

**Kim** Walker reminds us to reduce, recycle, and reuse.

Everyone who is related to you is your **kin**.

Ang Mo **Kio** is a hospital on Avenue 9 in Singapore.

I never hear the word **kip** or see it while reading but it has five entrees! Kip can mean half of a ton, a bed, a piece for a game called two-up in Australia, the smallest piece of money in Laos, and the list goes on. This word wins the prize for most entrees directly opposite the proportion of usage.

A **kit** can also be a small pocket violin.

Silly rabbit, **Kix** is a cereal, not a word.

A **koa** is a type of tree in Hawaii.

In Africa there are a variety of antelopes. Some antelopes are called **kob**.

I was the all-night disc-jockey on 93 **KOB**-FM Albuquerque when they were the number one radio station in New Mexico.

In South Africa, a hill can be called a **kop**.

A **kor** is a Hebrew measurement.

With a long "o", a **kos** is a measurement used in India.

In Liberia and the Ivory Coast, there is a group of people called the **Kru**.

Can a Kru ride his kob many kos to a kop as he plays his kit?

L

Here is a perfect example of an abbreviation evolving through usage to become its own word. A laboratory sounds like a place where mad scientists are plotting to take over the world. A **lab** sounds more like a place where humans are working to overcome disease and other earthly troubles.

Even as you read this, there are insects in southern Asia putting a sticky substance on different trees. This stuff is called **lac** and it is used in sealing wax.

A lass is a female child. A **lad** is a male child. Oingo Boingo is band of male grown-ups who play a song called *Only A Lad*. Find it. Play it. Dance.

In Papua New Guinea, the second biggest city is **Lae**.

To fall behind is to **lag**. A lag can also be a criminal.

If you're a lad or lass who is a lag, don't lag when you're on the **lam**. "Lam" can mean to be running from something.

**Lao** Tzu was a Chinese philosopher who lived about 2500 years ago. There are various ways to spell his name.

**Lap** can mean to eat in a hurry. Lap it up!

This one's from Latinland. Anyone find it on the map yet? THE WORLD BOOK DICTIONARY does not mention whether or not it's archaic. It's **lar** and it's a household god. THE AMERICAN HERITAGE DICTIONARY capitalizes the first letter and provides the same meaning.

While looking for Latinland, find Latvia. A **lat** is the name of a coin there. By the way, Latvia is a real country.

Charley **Lau** wrote <u>The Art of Hitting .300</u> despite having a .255 career batting average!

The best pronunciation of the word **law** is uttered by Inspector Jacques Clouseau.

Teacher Tangent #30
LAX stands for Los Angeles International Airport. I have flown in and out of it and parked and been ticketed and asked to move my car and waited for friends and family and curled around through the Airport Return and heard the speaker remind me that the white zone is for loading and unloading so often that LAX, like it or not, is a part of me. By the way, **lax** IS a word. It can mean careless. Security at LAX better not be lax.

Sometimes a good synonym for **lay** is arrangement.

A grassy field can be called a **lea**.

The past tense and past participle of lead is **led**.

Shelter can referred to as a **lee**.

A **leg** can also be a fielding position in Cricket.

A ring of flowers that goes over your head and rests on your shoulders is a **lei**. They are used with great frequency in Hawaii.

A **lek** is a place where male birds go to showoff to get a girlfriend. Bonus! In Albania, if you have 100 qintar, then you have a lek. Hey, how often do you see a word that starts with a "q" but is not followed with a "u", eh? Even THE AMERICAN HERITAGE DICTIONARY, mentions "qintar". Whoa.

**Lem** Barney, a defensive back for the Lions, is in Pro Football's Hall of Fame.

**Len** Dawson, quarterback for the Chiefs, is also in Pro Football's Hall of Fame.

**Leo** Tolstoy wrote War and Peace. There is not a Writer's Hall of Fame.

**Les** Cain won twelve games as a rookie for the Tigers in 1970.

Everyday, you have to **let** something go. My friend Jami Lula sings a great song called *Let It Go*. His web site is jamilula.com and his music can be sampled there.

In Romania, if you have a hundred bani, then you have a **leu**. You think I'm making this up.

In Bulgaria, if you have a hundred stotinki, you have a **lev**.

In June of 1961, **Lew** Krausse of the A's was seventeen years old and he shut out the Angels on three hits. It was his first pro baseball game!

Superman's main nemesis is Lex Luthor. In Latinville, **lex** is the word for law.

Next time you're lying in a lea, seeing images in the clouds; remember you read it here that "lea" can also be spelled **l-e-y**.

There's a country singer named **Lia**. Haven't heard her yet.

Sans an abbreviation, **lib** is a short word for liberation.

"Keep your **lid** on." Now, there's a rude phrase to make someone wait. Of course, maybe the person is being pushy. Pushy and rudeness are cousins who are always wrestling.

Don't **lie**.

I had an Aunt **Lil**. Also, this entry is a hip way of saying "little".

Don't give me any **lip** about lying.

Back to Latinelphia! They use **lis** to mean a lawsuit. Joe Lis was an outfielder for the Phillies. He also was a first baseman for the Twins, Indians, and an original member of the Mariners! This one is not bona fide.

The past tense for light is lighted. No, it's **lit**. Hey, they both work. Lit is a rock-n-roll band.

Anyone seen the new Lucy **Liu** movie?

What about the new **Liv** Tyler flick?

**Liz** Taylor's been in a few classic films.

The largest volcano on Earth is Mauna **Loa**.

114

I think of **lob** as a soft toss but our main reference uses a more exact definition concerning tennis. A tennis ball hit back in a high arc is a lob. The key word being "arc". The three letter words are helping to define each other now.

One of the first successful rappers was Tone **Loc**.

A **log** can be a piece of wood or a diary.

The next time you raise your hand to go use the restroom, bathroom, water closet, whatever you call it; try using the word **loo**. "Mister So and So? May I use the loo?" Keep a straight face. The best way to stay out of trouble when making a joke is to NOT make a face and let the others around you do the laughing. By the way, it's the British who use loo to mean potty.

You can use **lop** instead of cut, especially when it comes to discussing taking branches from trees.

There are lots of definitions for **lot**.

Teacher Tangent #31
While we're here, I want to point out something that many students take years to learn. I finally got it while attending the University of

New Mexico. Don't make "alot" one word. Keep them separated. Remember, "a" and "lot" are two words. Thanks a lot.

Even with its crease, I love my 1968 **Lou** Brock baseball card.

Did you know that **low** also means the sound a cow makes? Isn't that moo? When a cow moos, it is lowing.

A type of smoked salmon is **lox**. In New York City and Los Angeles, it is great fun to go out in the morning for fresh bagels and lox.

**Lud** is yet another brother in <u>Oh Say Can You Say</u> by Dr. Seuss. Lud is holding up all of his twenty brothers and they don't want him to sneeze.

It is finally coming to the attention of the adults that the backpacks kids are being asked to **lug** around are too heavy. Just because you can lift it doesn't mean you should carry it around long enough to damage your back.

Teacher Tangent #32
In Scotland, a chimney can be called a **lum**. Mike Lum was a left-handed outfielder for the Braves when Henry Aaron broke the all-time homerun record. Mike Lum went on to become a great pinch-hitter for the Reds during the years they were considered one of the

greatest teams ever. He's one of a handful of big leaguers to come from Hawaii.

In Britain, they sometimes call a dear friend, **luv**. Our back-up reference does not carry this entry.

In Latintown, **lux** means light and "lux" is the international unit of measurement telling an object's illumination. It's bona fide!

Time for Chemistry. Fear not! I got a cee in this subject, so I know what I'm talking about. Take some sodium hydroxide and potassium hydroxide. DO NOT mix them. Just understand that these can be used to make soap and that each can be called a **lye**.

(Remember to insert pun here)

(On second thought, don't).

M

Who is Queen **Mab**? Mercutio can tell you.

Hey dude, (and dudettes), before you were born, men who did not know each other might refer to one another as **Mac** as in "Hey Mac, get in the back of the line!" Dude has replaced Mac while Mac has been retooled. Have ever had a Big Mac? Mark McGwire has it as a nickname. It's an acronym for the Military Airlift Command in the United States Air Force. In England, it is a water resistant raincoat. I am writing this book on a Mac. Both reference dictionaries include this word even though it seems more like a name. Shouldn't all raincoats be water resistant?

**Mad** also has many meanings. I like to use it when describing a kind of love. I'm mad about baseball cards from the sixties.

Rita **Mae** Brown is a very successful writer.

**Mag** is slang for magazine. It can also mean to talk a lot or half a penny, depending where you are in England on a given day.

I often greet my friends with "Hey **man**, 'sup?"

**Mao** Tse Tung lived from 1893-1976. Was he the most powerful man in history? Find out.

Anyone found Latinopia on the **map** yet?

Teacher Tangent #33
Here's a great example of a three letter word that is easy to start using right away. Something is just right, maybe even perfect.

118

Someone comes along and messes it up. When a person or thing suffers an injury that makes the person or thing less than perfect, it has been marred. The root word is **mar**. When anyone is about to damage something, anything, or anyone, just ask them not to mar it. Your vocabulary will increase but unless they've read this book and understand what "mar" means, the damage will probably occur. Pass this book along while everything is still fine. Don't wait for damage to occur. If it's already too late, it's not your fault if that other person didn't take the time to learn a simple three letter word that could have saved everyone a lot of trouble.

More is **mas** in Spanish but mas is not a word in the English language.

My mother keeps a **mat** by every entrance to the house. So, wipe your feet!

I had a 1974 Maverick. I put over one hundred thousand miles on it. I called it "The **Mav**".

**Max** is short for Maxwell and max is short for maximum.

It's an oldie but a goodie. If April showers bring **May** flowers, what do Mayflowers bring? Pilgrims.

Charles **Mee** is a playwright.

I once got to chat with **Meg** Ryan at Jamba Juice. She couldn't believe I liked the taste of wheatgrass.

In the animated Japanese film, *Tonari no Totoro*, there are two sisters. One is Satsuki and the younger one is **Mei**. I haven't seen the movie but it is a classic in Japan.

Latinopolos is a place where **mel** means honey.

Teacher Tangent #34

A man named Mel would come to my classroom and facilitate a class discussion about getting along, how to handle teasing, avoiding trouble, peer pressure, etc., and the kids did not always know what to make of this retired guy waltzing in voluntarily. They didn't know what to make of him until he told a story about being in an airplane during World War II that got shot down. He parachuted out of the plane. When he landed he became a prisoner of war. He told great details of being a member of Stalag 17. The students always paid closer attention to him after that story. So did I. At one point, Mel and his fellow prisoners were ordered to march away from the camp and at a nameless point in the forest, while living on whatever nature could offer, they were told the war was over. He nearly starved to death but somehow found his way back to the United States and became a teacher and a principal. Things weren't always easy for him back in the USA though because he remained loyal to the Cleveland Indians.

More than one man is **men**.

I **met** Nolan Ryan once, in 1973, when he was no longer a Met.

Hawks are kept in a **mew**.

A **mho** is a measurement of electrical conductance.

Dr. **Mia** Wall gave me grammar and punctuation clarity while I wrote this book.

Does anyone play marbles any more? In case you do, the marble that you are shooting at is called the **mib**.

Short for middle is **mid**.

**Mij** Rothera is a photographer in Glasgow.

When you have one thousandth of an inch, you have a **mil**.

On February 19, 1978, I asked a girl named **Mim** if she'd be my girlfriend. She said yes and changed her mind the next day! I remember the date because I'm sentimental. In THE WORLD BOOK DICTIONARY, "mim" means to be primly quiet. THE AMERICAN HERITAGE DICTIONARY is mum on mim. February 19th is also Grandpa Brian's birthday. And Ashley's. And Smokey Robinson's. Wait, this is not a tangent!

THE WORLD BOOK DICTIONARY has an entry for **mir** with the first letter in lower case that says there were Russian farmers in the mid-1800's who formed a self-governing society. THE AMERICAN HERITAGE DICTIONARY agrees! On February 20, 1986, the Russians launched the first part of the Mir Space Station. It remained in orbit more than fifteen years. People lived on Mir and performed science experiments. Mir was a project where the United States worked closely with Russia. The success of Mir was because of the two country's cooperation. Did you notice the synchronistic coincidence with the dates mentioned in these last two paragraphs?

In New Zealand, there were a variety of birds that did not fly. They're now extinct. Scientists use the word **moa** to describe these long gone birds.

A lousy form of justice is **mob** justice.

Teacher Tangent #35

*The Mod Squad* was a TV show in the early seventies about police officers who were young, hip, slick, and cool. It was the last television show I watched before leaving for four years to Athens, Greece. There wasn't a whole lot of TV in Athens at the time. What I didn't know was, it was really good for me to have so few choices on the telly. I naturally did other things. My dad and I played a lot of backgammon and chess. My grades improved.

I meant to write that **mod** is short for modern.

**Moe** Berg was a big league catcher for five teams and a spy for the Allies in World War II.

To move along slowly is to **mog**. It's a verb that is spoken only in certain places but THE WORLD BOOK DICTIONARY does not specify where. THE AMERICAN HERITAGE DICTIONARY does not include mog. Perhaps they are being mog in adding it.

Ye Rin **Mok** was born in Korea and is now a photographer in Los Angeles. Smile!

My **mom** was born in 1934 in Halontown, Iowa. The population has fluctuated over the years between a hundred fifty and two hundred fifty people. The town's claim to fame is that every year on June 21st (the longest day of the year), the sun sets exactly between the rails on the train track.

There are several entrees for **mon**. Use the one that describes people who live in southeastern Burma but are not Burmese. It might come in handy if you're on Jeopardy.

I love when toddlers **moo** like a cow. If you've never played farm animal sound games with the wee folk, give it a try.

Get the **mop** and mop. English is fun when the verb and noun match so perfectly.

In our main reference, **mor** is lousy soil. Our other dictionary comes clean by rinsing out mor.

**Mos** Def is most definitely a rapper and an actor.

Don't pronounce the tee for this next noun. Hopefully, critics will think this paragraph is **mot**, which is somewhere between witty and clever. Or they may want to use it as mor. Then we won't have to **mow** and can play in the **mud** instead.

Sometimes a noun, sometimes a verb; to **mug** is to make faces.

Remain **mum** about whom you think has an ugly mug.

The Scottish use **mun** to mean must. Our American reference does not have this entry.

A dog is sometimes called a mutt. Someone somewhere misspelled it and hence, **mut**, has become acceptable. Ut-oh, THE AMERICAN HERITAGE DICTIONARY shuns this thought. My friend Jon Mersel, despite not having a dog, accepts both spellings.

N

To catch something quickly is to **nab** it.

The Scottish use **nae** to mean no.

If you are constantly criticizing someone, you're a **nag**. Don't nag. No one likes a nag. Quit naggin'. You here me? Don't make me come off this page and teach you a lesson about nagging. Nagging never did anyone any good anyhow. So, knock it off. Now, go and get me a doughnut. Hurry up about it. Don't dawdle. Move it. Why do I have to tell you more than once? Make sure it's got jelly in the middle and it's fresh. You always bring the stale one. Who taught you how to pick a doughnut anyway? Never mind, I'll get it myself.

**Nam** is short for Viet Nam. My dad proudly served there. He was at Cam Ranh Bay from October of 1969 to October of 1970.

You know there are many kinds of cars. Well, there are many kinds of ships, too. Five hundred years ago, a **nao** was a type of sailing ship. It was small but sturdy. The Santa Maria, which was the flagship for Christopher Columbus when he sailed the ocean blue in 1492, was a nao.

I always feel better after a **nap**.

If near is the opposite of far, is fear the opposite of **nar**? No, nar is not a word.

There is a rapper named **Nas**.

A kind of demon or genie, in both Thailand and Burma, is called a **nat**.

Dana S. **Nau** is a Professor at the University of Maryland.

It's called a **nay** vote when you vote against a proposition.

**Ned** can throw a knucklecurve with a whiffleball better than anyone in the universe.

This one is from France and has to do with being born. If your teacher is a woman who is recently married and changed her name, use **nee**. Say her new last name is Jones and her maiden name was Garcia. In order for everyone to adjust to the new last name, it is proper to say "Mrs. Jones nee Garcia".

THE WORLD BOOK DICTIONARY recognizes a word from the Afrikaans language. This language is spoken in the Republic of South Africa by about eight million people. South Africa is a long way from America, so it is understandable why THE AMERICAN HERITAGE DICTIONARY does not include it. The word is **nek** and it is the low ridge between two hills.

Robb **Nen** was a relief pitcher for three teams and he always wore #31.

If **Neo** from *The Matrix* was a baseball player, he'd be #1.

You or someone you know gets a paycheck. The total amount earned is gross. After taxes and other deductions are subtracted, whatever remains is **net**. The old joke is "My net is gross."

What's **new**?

Most everyone I know calls the point of a pen the tip. While not incorrect, it is more exact to call the point of a pen a **nib**.

When cutting stone, a mallet or a chisel helps chip away bigger pieces but sometimes you might want to **nig**. This verb means to cut with finer detail using a sharp-pointed hammer. THE AMERICAN HERITAGE DICTIONARY has nil on nig.

Another word for nothing is **nil**.

Ask your math teacher if you can play **nim**.

The diaries of Anais **Nin** have been published!

**Nip** has many definitions. Jack Frost should register it as his trademark before someone else takes it.

When a louse lays an egg, it's called a **nit**.

It's an interjection? The word is **nix**. I hear it as a verb meaning that something will be stopped or changed in the future. For example, "We will go to the mall and nix plans to exercise."

Cribbage experts may recognize **nob** as part of that game. Wealthy British people are sometimes called nobs. A nob can be a bald head.

Can you write a sentence about a wealthy bald British person (man or woman) playing Cribbage? If you are flinching at the idea of a bald woman, check out the first *Star Trek* movie, even though earlier I told you to skip it.

To **nod** your head is to say yes or it means you're falling asleep. Hopefully the teacher is asking you if you're falling asleep and one nod can serve the purpose for both meanings.

**Noe** Valley is a neighborhood in San Francisco.

A **nog** can be a peg. It is also short for eggnog.

There is an ancient Japanese dance called **Noh**. It is still performed today by both professionals and amateurs. The show is a performance is a mixture of dance, theater, poetry and music. If you're ever in Tokyo, check out a show.

**Noi** was a waitress at Tommy Tang's restaurant on Melrose in Los Angeles. I was a busboy.

I play basketball with a great guy named Non. Now, **non** is not its own word but is a prefix for more than fifteen hundred words. Always a bridesmaid, never a bride.

World Book, Inc., neither collaborated on, **nor** endorses this book, and therefore cannot attest to the accuracy of its contents.

Please do **not** make silly faces for the class photo. I like them but if we do it, then all the classes will want to and chaos will ensue.

**Now**, on with the countdown.

In ancient Rome, the goddess of night was **Nox**.

A lump is a **nub**.

Karen Armstrong, a former **nun**, is one of my favorite writers.

Is there a distinction between being a fool and a **nut**?

**Nuv** Yug is an Indian American organization in North Carolina that celebrates the culture of India.

**Nux** Vomica is the name of a homeopathic medicine. Vomica? I ain't taking any.

Rich **Nye** was a lefty pitcher for the Cubs in the late sixties.

In ancient Greece, the goddess of night was **Nyx**. Then the Romans came in and nixed the Greeks power but kept the ideas of the gods (among other things). Athena became Venus. Apollo became Jupiter. Nyx became Nox.

O

An **oaf** is a clumsy person. Do you have a great story about falling down and laughing hard at yourself? My younger brother can tell you several about me.

The wood of an **oak** tree is strong and hard.

**Oar** can be both a noun and a verb. You row a boat with an oar. As verbs, "row" and "oar" are synonyms. Oar oar oar your boat, gently with your oar. Orally orally orally orally, my English teacher screams.

For the **oat** entry, a short story: When my son was two and a half, he pronounced oatmeal with three syllables. He said "o tee mall" with the accent on the first letter. I like how he said it so much that I now call our local shopping mall Otimall.

To be a king in Nigeria is to be an **oba**! Bonus: If you are ever hungry in downtown Portland, Oregon, I highly recommend Oba, a restaurant on 12th Avenue in the Pearl District. Ask for Mike.

Is Obi-wan one name or is it a first name and a middle name? In real life, an **obi** is a sash worn by Japanese people. It fits something like a belt but is tied around the back.

When you are in the Andes Mountains of South America, you might taste an **oca**. It's the root of a plant, also called "oca", that has yellow flowers.

Oh, no! It's interjection time! When the Scottish or Irish say "oh", they spell it o-c-h. Hold on. People don't spell when they utter words, unless they don't want children to hear. Anyway, och is oh. THE WORLD BOOK DICTIONARY says they are pronounced the same. THE AMERICAN HERITAGE DICTIONARY has zero on och.

I had a friend in high school named Bill W. (No, not that Bill W.) He loved to draw a small cartoon character called an **ock**. They are not real and neither is the word but he drew thousands of these little round creatures on notebooks, on his school work, everywhere. Ocks populated his world.

**Odd** is quirkier than strange. To be odd suggests there's hope. To be strange is to be potentially dangerous. Odd can be figured out. Strange feels like one should get away quickly.

A lyrical poem is an **ode**. Writers often title a piece of work to someone or some thing by calling it an ode, such as *Ode to Billie Joe*. Do they still make songs that are complete stories?

**Odo** is a great character in the Star Trek universe and the name of a Catholic saint. But, it's not in any dictionary.

**Ody** Saban is a female artist who was born in Turkey.

An archaic preposition and adverb that lives on only in poems is **o'er** which stands for over.

"They're **off**!" is said excitedly at the beginning of a race. Off in this case means "on the way". Off can mean on? Yes!

When we say "often", the tee is not pronounced, but in the word **oft**, which means often, the tee is pronounced. Porque?

A physicist from Germany was named Ohm and he is remembered today in the electricity business whenever electrical resistance is measured. Electrical resistance is measured in ohms. It is possible to have only one **ohm**.

Not sure whether we should play the interjection fanfare or not. Both reference dictionaries say **oho** is an interjection used when someone is surprised or joyous. Perhaps you yahoo but does anyone oho?

Here's a powerful three-letter word. **Oil**. It is an integral part of our energy system. Many fight to keep it that way. Many try to change it.

I lived in Izmir, Turkey when I was two until I was six. I lived in Athens, Greece from ages thirteen to seventeen. In both countries an **oka** is a weight of measurement just under three pounds. I've never been to Quebec, Canada. There is a village there in which monks make cheese. The village is called Oka. So is the cheese. Could a Greek order an oka of Oka? Oho.

Oka is also called **oke**. Does it go with Coke? Neither go with my American dictionary.

Another way of saying and writing old is **ole**.

The **Omo** Valley is in Ethiopia.

**One** of the most underrated comedians is Wakko Warner.

Teacher Tangent #36

While not a bona fide word, **ong** is used at the beginning of a mantra in Kundalini Yoga. It's head practitioner is Yogi Bhajan. He once walked by me as I was leaning against a wall and asked, "Who is this Charlie Chaplin character?" It is the best compliment I can imagine.

Let's not forget Yoko **Ono**.

A slang word for money in Britain is **oof**.

Interjection time! This time the entry is **ooh**. Does anyone not use that one? Characters on TV use "ooh" right after someone's crashed. Wincing faces usually accompany "ooh".

In Holland and other places where Dutch is the main language, **oom** is used before the name of an elderly person as a sign of love and respect. Capitalize the first letter and "Oom" is a word for uncle in Afrikaans. Oom is not a part of American English.

Many mistakes? Use "oops". For one mistake, use **oop**. Oops. Wrong again. Oop is not a word.

An archaic way to say open is to say **ope**.

Highlight this entry. It is yet another easy word to start using. I guarantee that your teacher will think you're smarter. Sometimes you say, "I choose green." or "I choose the big one." or "I choose chocolate." Choose the word **opt** in place of "choose". When you opt for "opt", you'll be thought of as genius. The people marking your report cards will give the highest grades possible. This could last until your first year of college. Professors see right through this malarkey.

Some of you who have been looking for the country of Latinberg claim you can't find it on any map. Look harder. What does that mean? Look harder? How does one increase focus of one's eyes? Should I move the map closer to my face? Perhaps the missing piece should take some of the responsibility in being found by lighting up or beeping. Anyway, in Latin, wherever it is, **ora** is the plural of "os". Bonus: I have a friend named Ora.

Another easy three-letter word for you to incorporate into your vocabulary is **orb**. It's anything that is shaped like a ball. While baseorb and basketorb may not sound like fun, simply playing catch with an orb sounds like you are doing science. By the way, a football is not an orb.

The killer whale is an **orc**. There are several kinds of orcs, they are all marine mammals.

If you have a hundred ores, you have a Norwegian krone. People also go **ore** mining. It's hard work. If you ever find yourself doing any kind of mining, make sure you're getting paid well, and wear a hat.

A member of Hockey's Hall Of Fame, from the Boston Bruins, Number Four, Bobby **Orr**!

Can you play the **oud**? You probably can if you know how to play the lute.

The French word for yes is **oui** and it's pronounced like the English "we".

Speak of the devil, **our** is the possessive form of "we".

Teacher Tangent #37

Maybe you've heard the phrase, "When one door closes, another is being opened." Another way to think about it is, if you are **out** one place, you are in another. When I am outside my house, I am usually in the rain because I live in Portland. When I am out of cookies, I am in my craving for sugar. We could go on and on and I think I will. When I am out of money, I am in need of more. When I am out of sight from the police, I usually am in the intersection making an illegal u-turn.

The plural of ovum is **ova**.

William Shakespeare wrote "Neither a borrower nor a lender be." He's telling us that it's no fun to **owe** money and even though lending money may feel powerful, after awhile, it's not fun to have others owe you money either.

An **owl** is not the only thing that is an owl. There are pigeons that look like owls and they are also called owls. Oho.

An important grammar lesson is to recognize that to possess and to **own** are the same thing. It's not always true in the real world but it is when it comes to the English language.

Very rarely, **owt** is used for ought. It's not bona fide.

This one is not English but I thought you'd like to know that **oxi** means "no" in Greek.

**Oxo** is an obscure band but not a word.

**Oxy** has something to do with oxen and also has to do with oxygen. THE AMERICAN HERITAGE DICTIONARY claims it is only a prefix. I'm staying out of this one.

A grandchild to someone who speaks Spanish is an oy which can also be spelled **oye**. This is also true in Scotland! But it's not a bona fide word in English.

**Ozo** is another obscure band and also not a word.

P

Does anyone use **pad** to mean their place of residence anymore?

It's interjection time! **Pah** is what people say when they don't believe you or think something is disgusting.

A buddy, a friend, a chum, a comrade, is also a **pal**.

I have a cousin in Texas named **Pam**.

If it's true that every book needs a villain, here's mine. In the movie biz, the camera person may want to follow the action. Moving the camera to follow the action is to **pan**. You may hear the director say, "After the explosion, pan over to see the reaction of the villain."

Food made to be so soft that babies can eat it is called **pap**.

In golf, **par** is used a lot but it's okay to use it anytime you wish to speak of equality.

A certain type of dance in France is called **pas**. As with many French words, don't sound out the last letter. Hey, THE AMERICAN HERITAGE DICTIONARY has this entry!

If you have actually incorporated some of these words into your personal vernacular, **pat** yourself on the back.

When someone is finished with something in Hawaii, they may use the word **pau** to signal they're done. Alas, THE AMERICAN HERITAGE DICTIONARY, does not have this definition. It does mention that Pau is a town of nearly 84,000 people in France.

A dog with a bandage wrapped around one foot limps into a bar and orders a drink. The bartender doesn't recognize the dog but pours him a drink anyway. The dog slurps his drink. The bartender prods him by saying, "You're not from around here. Is there anything I can help with you with?" The dog shows the bartender his bandage and says, "I'm looking for the man who shot my **paw**."

In Latinia, peace is **pax**. In the Roman Catholic Church, it is a small kiss from the clergy during communion. The Greeks had a goddess for peace named Irene. When the Romans took over, they kept the idea but changed the name to Pax.

I was twelve and standing in a pizza joint in Albuquerque, New Mexico. A sign on the wall seared its message into me. It said, "In God we trust, all others **pay** cash."

Octavio **Paz** of Mexico won the 1990 Nobel Prize for Literature. Read his work.

In an early Woody Allen movie called *Take The Money And Run*, there's a scene where a criminal, his wife, and their daughter sit down to dinner. The three of them have to split one **pea**.

There are many ways to tell someone you're off to the bathroom but **pee** is one of the most interesting. It can be a noun or a verb. My experience tells me it is not an inappropriate word. Moms use it all the time. I've heard people in business settings use it without being scolded but my wife works in a corporate office and she disagrees with me. She says no one would say it in her office. Perhaps pee is the dividing line between appropriate and inappropriate. It must be somewhat naughty because it's not in THE WORLD BOOK DICTIONARY and I wouldn't use it when asking a restaurant employee where the bathroom is. Perhaps it is a word that is still evolving. Listen to how people use it. Does it create a reaction like the stronger curse words or are the people around you fine with it? Bonus nonsense: P-e-e is how to spell the letter "p".

A **peg** is a place to hang your coat and it is a great 70's song by Steely Dan.

The seventeenth letter of the Hebrew alphabet is **peh**. Pronounce it like the word "pay".

When I was a kid, it bugged me that the sounds of **pen** and pin were so close. You mean a writing pen or a stick in the wall pin? It was my first lesson in the importance of enunciation. Today, pens aren't just pens. There are gel pens and Bic pens and erasable pens. Pins can be tacks or, better yet, pushpins.

Synonyms for **pep** include energy, force, and vigor.

When I teach word problems in math, we look for key words that help tell which operation (add, subtract, multiply, divide) to use. If you see **per** in a word problem, it means either multiply or divide. If you can't tell, choose division.

This entry rhymes with tease. The word is **pes** and it has to do with the back of one of your feet.

I had a **pet** named Basia. She was my cat when I lived alone in Hollywood and when I moved slightly west to a one bedroom apartment near Olympic and La Cienega in Los Angeles. I miss her.

**Pew** is not smelling something stinky, it's a place to sit in church.

Did you bring enough **Pez** for everyone?

The twenty-first letter of the Greek alphabet is **phi**.

The entry for **pia** suggests that it has something to do with an area around the brain and spinal cord. Another has to do with a nutritious Polynesian herb.

A **pic** is the weapon used on a bull by a picador.

Teacher Tangent #38

When you read **pie**, you think of dessert but there are also meat pies, vegetable pies, and my least favorite, chicken pot pie. When my dad was in Viet Nam, I lived with my mom and two brothers in Mankato, Minnesota. My mom brought out chicken pot pies and I cringed. It is easy to say now that I ate them to support my mom who was in turn supporting my dad who was following the orders of his Commander-In-Chief. Yes, I was eating chicken pot pie to aid my country but I haven't had one since.

Teacher Tangent #39

In 2002, I had a fourth grade class and we had so much fun learning idioms. Let me tell you, idioms can drive you up the wall. If one of my former students is reading this, we missed one. "In a **pig**'s eye!" is a firm stand to not do something. Are you ever going to smoke? In a pig's eye! I actually did smoke in fifth grade and my mom caught me. She told me I had two choices. She could tell my dad or she would take charge of punishing me. Of course, I let my sweet mother handle the situation. Well, I had never seen her so angry and she beat the habit of smoking out of me. She whipped me harder than my father ever did. Sorry mom. At least she didn't force me to eat chicken pot pie.

Did you know that the stick in the hole holding up the triangle flag in golf is called a **pin**? Me neither.

I also didn't know that a **pip** is what you call one of those spots on a pair of dice or on a deck of cards.

The **Pit** is the name of a basketball arena in Albuquerque, New Mexico. There are more than a dozen other definitions for pit but the main one, a hole in the ground, suffices for most of the rest.

The Italians give us an adverb for the music world. It is **piu**. It means more. More what I don't know. As long as it's not chicken pot pie. This foreign word is in THE AMERICAN HERITAGE DICTIONARY!

Would someone else like to try and create an entry for **ply**?

*Invasion of the Body Snatchers* is a movie about the true story of aliens taking over the Earth. When you go to sleep at night, check every room in your house, go around the outside of it, and make sure that no one has placed a **pod** anywhere. Inside the pod is an alien who takes on all your physical features but does not take on your charming personality. In the morning, the alien takes your place because you...well, you disappear. Like I said before, it's completely true! If you don't believe me, ask your parents. They'll back my story. Another definition of "pod" is that it can be a small group of seals or whales.

There is a theory that Edgar Allen **Poe** was voted to death.

There is game called Pogs. It is played with pogs. I own some pogs. If I only had one, I would have a **pog**. But my reference dictionaries do not include pog! It is not a bona fide word.

You think "pooh" is a bear but it's really an interjection suggesting you don't believe something and **poh** is alternative way to spell such negativity. THE AMERICAN HERITAGE DICTIONARY does not believe in poh. Jon Mersel does.

When you are in Hawaii, eat some **poi**.

An informal word for politician is **pol**. There are other words for politicians that we won't go into here. Believe it or not, some pols get into politics because they wish to be servants to the public. Really.

Sometimes in Australia, there are British immigrants. They are referred to as poms. I do not know if calling someone a **pom** is derogatory. Our American reference denied this entry.

How can **poo** not be in either of my reference dictionaries? Is it because someone a long time ago thought it was too close to poop? Toddlers say "poo" don't they? Unfortunately, I entered p-o-o on Google to see if these letters worked as a word. They did! The web sites I found? They stunk.

Do not **pop** gum in my class. Do not pop balloons, either. Otherwise, there'll be a pop quiz.

I like the definition of **pot** that is about being ruined. If I start eating only cake and gambling and staying up all night driving forklifts in the snow, my life will soon go to pot.

On the *Batman* TV show in the sixties, it was always fun when he was fighting and **POW!** would flash on the screen.

A pock is a sore on the body. More than one pock? That's **pox**.

Among other things, a **pro** is someone who earns money.

Adults are always telling children to mind their own business. Well, if you go against that, if you like minding other people's business, you like to **pry**.

A **pub** is a place where adults can drink alcohol. Generally, we say "bar" in the United States and "pub" is more common in England.

In Russia, a little more than thirty-six pounds is a "pood". While p-u-d is an alternative spelling, THE AMERICAN HERITAGE DICTIONARY does not include **pud** as an entry. Poo.

Besides being a dog, a **pug** is a verb in the brick making business that has to with mixing ingredients to make bricks.

When a word has more than one meaning and the different meanings make a joke, it's called a **pun**. Punoftheday is a very funny web site.

A **pup** is a baby dog and sometimes it is used by older men when they speak of younger men.

Purr can also be **pur**, though I never knew a cat that stopped at the first "r". Every American English teacher could and should mark you wrong if you use this entry.

Some sores have a liquidy mixture of yellow and white that oozes out. That's **pus**. Some think it's gross. Some think it's fun.

I misplace my keys and my wallet, then drive everyone crazy trying to find where I **put** them.

In French, hill is **puy**. It's not a word in English.

Neither is this one. In Burma, there is a big outdoor show that has a lot of singing, dancing, comedy, and drama. This big show is called a **pwe**.

Also in Burma, if you have one hundred **pya**, you have a kyat. I don't know how many pyas it takes to go to the pwe. This one, by the way, is in BOTH of our dictionaries.

So is this one. At the British mint (the place where money is made) they have special coin box called a **pyx**.

Q

Do you recall "kat" is a bush in Africa and Arabia that has a leaf that some people chew? THE WORLD BOOK DICTIONARY says we can use **qat** for kat. THE AMERICAN HERITAGE DICTIONARY does not acknowledge kat or qat. How about that?

**Qon** is a city in Iran.

An adjective that describes filling in for someone or something is **qua**. A substitute teacher is your qua teacher.

Even though it's not English, **que** is here because it is used so often in Southern California and other parts of the USA. It is the Spanish word for "what".

A term for normal is status **quo**. Now, "status" can be it's own word but "quo" cannot be? If "quo" cannot be alone, shouldn't it be "statusquo"? Hey, "quo" also shows up in "quid pro quo" and "terminus a quo" yet it cannot stand alone. Fine. Be that way. Alright already. So are you but what am I?

R

Teacher Tangent #40

<u>Johnny Tremain</u> by Esther Forbes is a book that Mrs. Benningfield read to us in fifth grade. I vividly remember the boy burning his hand. A year after she read it to us, I read it again, and felt proud to finish it. When I began teaching fifth grade, I encouraged students to read this book and no one would touch it. There were no pictures, the print was small, and the action moved too slowly. Fine, then, I'll be like Mrs. Benningfield and read it to them. Same problem. No one liked it. Not even me. We couldn't make it to the second chapter. Then Mrs. Marge Simpson began home schooling her son Bart Simpson on television. She made Bart read <u>Johnny Tremain</u>. He liked it and got something out of it. Using this new connection, I challenged one of my struggling students who happen to love *The Simpsons* to be like Bart and read <u>Johnny Tremain</u>. He did and he gave a great book report about it. I was never more proud as a teacher. Johnny Tremain makes friends with an older boy at the start of the Revolutionary War. The boy's name is **Rab**.

For awhile, **rad** was a trendy word. It was short for radical. Young people were down with "rad". Rad is no longer hip. Scientists though have always been chummy with rad because they get to play with radiation. A rad is a unit of measuring radiation.

Teacher Tangent #41

I had a landlady in Los Angeles who leased a one bedroom apartment to me for four hundred fifty dollars a month for seven years. Her benevolence provided me the opportunity to eat at restaurants more often, make car payments, but more importantly, I could afford to go back to school and get a fancy degree. When she died, the guy in charge of her estate, the incomparable Steve Conti, let me go into her house and choose a piece of furniture for myself. I chose her writing desk with the fold down door. Many old people leave us everyday and I have no connection to them. But I see and feel her kindness every day. Her name was **Rae**.

It's always a sad moment when a favorite shirt becomes a **rag**.

It's interjection time! Yippee! Let's do cartwheels. Now holding auditions for interjection cheerleaders. Must be able to **rah**. Rah-rah-sis-boom-bah. Rah is short for hurrah.

In India, political power is **raj**.

A male sheep is a **ram**.

The past tense of run is **ran** but Ran is also a sea goddess from Scandinavia who caught drowning men in her net.

Xue Son **Rao** is a research scientist at the National University of Singapore.

Rock-n-roll wouldn't last. That's what many people thought in the late fifties. **Rap** would not last. That's what many people thought in the eighties and deep into the nineties. What really won't last? Peace and anything with the word collectible on it.

In Ethiopia, a prince, governor, or chief can be called a **ras**.

One of my favorite theme songs is from the television show *The **Rat** Patrol*. They weren't rats or cats looking for rats. They were soldiers in North Africa fighting against the Nazis.

In the 70's, Doug **Rau** won eighty games for the Dodgers.

I have a good friend who spent a couple of years getting in touch with his deepest pains and hurts. He earned a nickname during that period of time. We called him **Raw**.

The Scottish use **rax** to mean to stretch or reach out.

Teacher Tangent #42

When I was a teenager in Greece, my friend Tom Jones and I were snorkeling. I was looking down from the surface about six feet above Tom who was skimming along the sandy floor. Suddenly, a **ray** rose out of the sand close to Tom. We watched it swim away. It was a magnificent moment.

Ran **Raz** is a mathematics whiz in Israel. He may even be a genius!

Chris **Rea** had a hit song in the USA back in 1979. He's much more popular in Europe.

An informal term for rebel is **reb**.

**Red** is the top color of a rainbow.

**Ref** is short for referee.

**Reg** is short for Reggie which is short for Reginald. Elton John's real name is Reginald Dwight.

The Portuguese had money called a real. The plural was reis. Nine of them made one United States cent. It was okay to spell "reis" without the final letter and just have **rei**. The Brazilians have the same story except it took eighteen reis to make a cent. Our back-up reference has no deposits of this type.

Vitold **Rek** is a jazz musician from Poland who plays the double bass.

In 1974, Eric **Rel** was my teammate on the Bears. We won one game.

A **rem** is the unit of measurement in counting absorbed radiation. R.E.M. is a great band from Georgia. Remember my friend Raw?˜ He loves R.E.M.

Are **Ren** and Stimpy still around?

There are several definitions for **rep** including another radiation one but the place you here it the most is in a weight room. A rep is one count of lifting a weight.

I've never seen it used before but **res** is a noun in the law business. Rhymes with "breeze".

To **ret** is the action of rotting in moisture.

When you are sitting in a parked car, does the driver sometimes push on the gas pedal making the engine louder even though you're not going anywhere? That's revving the engine and **rev** is short for "revolution". In this instance, revolution has to do with a mechanical circle.

Thornton Wilder won a Pulitzer Prize in 1927 for his book, <u>The Bridge of San Luis **Rey**</u>.

The **Rex** Allen Museum is in Willcox, Arizona.

While not bona fide, **rez** is sometimes short for "reservation".

The seventeenth letter of the Greek alphabet is **rho**.

Each of my students make a very detailed geography dictionary. It enhances our reading skills because so many authors write beautiful scenes with knolls, ravines, inlets, fjords, deltas, tributaries, washes, straits, et cetera. THE WORLD BOOK DICTIONARY, on page 1793, offers that a **ria** is "an arm of the sea that gradually becomes shallower inland" Now, I know all of you saved the dictionary you made in my class so please go back and add this entry. What are you looking at me like that for? You think I'm ribbin' ya? THE

AMERICAN HERITAGE DICTIONARY does not support my claim. Perhaps they figured the word has not been used since 1793. You're off the hook.

To **rib** someone is to tease them.

**Ric** Ocasek was the lead singer of The Cars. I saw them open for Styx!

Got too much stuff? Get **rid** of some.

**Rie** Munoz is an artist in Juneau, Alaska.

The **Rif** Mountains are in Morocco.

A fun synonym for truck is **rig**.

Kryvyy **Rih** is a city in the Ukraine.

Ryf Van **Rij** is an actor who played Detective Rafe on *The Sentinel*.

The oval bar holding the net on a basketball hoop is a **rim**.

If it's 1950 and you're in Japan, the coin you are spending might be called a **rin**.

River in Spanish is **rio**.

.

When my son was born, the school I was teaching at sold used children's books for a dollar each. I bought a lot of them. When he would **rip** the pages, I didn't fret. He didn't do it very often.

To steal is to take what is not yours. To **rob** is to take what is not yours through force or other intimidating methods.

**Rod** has several meanings. A divining rod is a stick shaped like a "y" and leads one to water.

Fish eggs are **roe**. I was a bartender at a sushi restaurant and the chefs would slide samples down my way. Eel became a favorite. Roe can also be a European deer. I never worked at a venison restaurant.

Roger Shank created the cover of this book. I call him **Rog**.

A **Rom** is a gypsy male.

Before the *Harry Potter* movies started rolling out, there was a boy in my class who easily could have been cast as the lead. He loved the books and it was always fun to walk over to him and pretend I was Snape. I would give him dirty looks, say mean things, and bad-mouth Gryffindor. He either laughed or began acting like Harry. I don't know if he learned anything in my class but we had a good time. His name was, and still is, **Ron**.

THE WORLD BOOK DICTIONARY says 'roo is an appropriate term for kangaroo. THE AMERICAN HERITAGE DICTIONARY does not. But, just this once, I went to THE COMPACT OXFORD ENGLISH DICTIONARY, to break the tie. It's there! Roo lives! To complicate things, our tie-breaking dictionary does not use the apostrophe.

Floss! Don't let your teeth **rot**.

A loud fight is a **row**.

**Roy** Gilbert was my dad's friend. He and Sylvia could really cut a rug.

**Roz** is the great librarian at Castle Heights Elementary School in Los Angeles. Since my class was just across the hall from the library, I often ran in and asked for a book that had pictures of whatever I was teaching at that moment. She found books for me instantly. She's faster than DSL.

When you're playing competitive sports and you win, do not **rub** it in the loser's face. It's okay to celebrate victory but learn not to taunt.

Haven't had an archaic word in awhile. In the olden days, **rud** could mean a reddish color. In Norwegian, it has to do with a pasture. The AMERICAN HERITAGE DICTIONARY mentions that the Hari Rud is a river in the Middle East.

He'll **rue** the day he gambled away that money. "Rue" means to regret.

When a man wears a hairpiece, it's okay to call it a **rug**, the hairpiece, not the man, and you may not wish to do it to his face.

**Ruj** Ujjin is a medical doctor in Georgia.

You know how all alcoholic beverages can be called booze? You can also call it **rum**, although rum is also a specific type of alcohol.

Diarrhea is sometimes called the runs. Is it possible to have diarrhea in the singular? Maybe that's what people mean when they say "Gotta **run**."

To be stuck in a **rut** means it's hard to find motivation.

A Fennoscandian rug is called a **rya**.

Sometimes the waiter wants to know if you want white, wheat, or **rye**. Rye is a plant with many uses. It's even in booze! Order up a ham on rye and some rye whiskey and duck before your parent or guardian quickly gives you your least favorite consequence.

S

**Sab** is not in the dictionary! My mom used that word when she was rubbing a greasy concoction from a tube on a boo-boo. That was sab. No? It was "salve" and the ell is not pronounced. The last vowel is silent. The vee simply sounded like a "b" to me.

As near as I can figure, a sack is a man-made item that carries things but **sac** is for an organic holder of things. A bladder is a sac.

To be **sad** too long is to be depressed.

In Scotland, so is **sae**.

A good synonym for **sag** is droop.

At the pharmacy, salt can be **sal**.

As a junior in high school, my closest friend was **Sam** Logan. His favorite singer was Olivia Newton-John and she came out with a song called *Sam*. It blew our minds that she was crooning to him! That coincidence still amazes me. Today, Sam is very proud of his nonprofit organization called Make A Difference USA. It helps a variety of people in need. Check it out at makeadifferenceusa.com.

The word **san** is in our main reference. "San" is an informal word for "sanatorium", which is not to be confused with "sanitarium". THE AMERICAN HERITAGE DICTIONARY also has "san" but with a completely different meaning having to do with Africa.

Expensive syrup in real glass is derived from **sap** that comes out of trees. I don't mind paying the extra money. But I do mind the prior paragraph. I've written it five different which ways and still can't make heads or tails of it.

Jack Sprat **sat** on his hat and that was that.

In Viet Nam, if you have a hundred **sau**, you have a dong.

A wise saying or proverb can be called a **saw**.

**Sax** is not just short for saxophone, it's also a roofing tool.

**Say**, would you forgive me for going out of order in this paragraph?

He joined the navy to **see** the world.

But what did he see?

He saw the **sea**.

The **Saz** is sort of, kind of, like a guitar that is made and played in Turkey.

Remember Geb, who could also be called Keb, and was married to Nut? Geb, who also could be called Keb, can also be called **Seb**. Perhaps this Egyptian god family will get a reality TV show and we can see how deities get through the day.

Despite being entered in both dictionaries in connection with wine and champagne, neither reference mentions that it is also slang for what people often yell at each other. "Wait a **sec**!"

**See**? See "Sea".

A segregationist is a person who believes that people of different races should live apart. For short, a segregationist can be called a **seg** and apparently it's not considered a slur. THE AMERICAN HERITAGE DICTIONARY did not have this entry.

There are a couple of terrific web sites about the **sei** whale.

A word used for some coins in Japan, Indonesia, and Kampuchea is **sen**.

In India, things can be measured in sers. A **ser** is about two pounds. Our American reference does not include this one.

As a kid, one of my chores was to **set** the table. I hardly had any chores. My mom believed I should have lots of time to be a kid. Life was going to be tough enough as an adult so she let me enjoy being young. Did I have a great mom or what? She also made the world's best iced tea. My childhood friends still remember it.

Teacher Tangent #43

A teacher's enthusiasm can implant itself like nothing else. I cannot remember the name, but an English teacher who loved Mark Twain was reading an excerpt and going guffaw over a scene in which Huck Finn was dressed like a girl while trying to impress a lady with his ability to **sew**. What gave away that Huck wasn't a girl was that he would move the needle to the thread instead of holding the needle still and guiding the thread into the tiny oval shape. Now, I was bored to tears, but this teacher went on and on about how funny this scene was and wouldn't you know, years later in college, I had to read that whole book and when I got to that scene, I not only laughed and enjoyed that scene in particular, but had a connection with that teacher who was now long out of my life. Perhaps this paragraph is more for the teachers in the crowd. Shine your light even when the audience is burned out. You never know when their little light bulb will use your spark.

**Sex** doesn't always mean sex. At times it simply means gender.

Jeffrey **Sez** is a rock band in Canada.

Al Green had a hit record called *Sha La La (Make Me Happy)*.

Speaking of genders, **she** means female.

Remember Nut? She was a goddess of the sky and her back was arched. A god named **Shu**, god of the air, was represented by outstretched arms. Shu supported Nut.

Teacher Tangent #44

When toddlers are acting **shy**, don't force them not to be. They are going through a natural phase of development. I know there is no scientific data but one theory is that whatever is forced upon a child in the toddler days goes into an account which gets paid back double to the parent during the teenage years.

A synonym for kin is **sib**. What is kin? Go back and look.

Sometimes writers who want to show-off use **sic** and it has to do with repeating something that was formerly written. Now that redundancy is unpopular, "sic" will be archaic. But wait, I read once that there is no such thing as original thought, therefore, everything is redundant. This is becoming a tangent. Let's tiptoe out of this paragraph.

**Sid** Caesar was a great comedian.

Thor was not married to Nut though perhaps they met at a deity party. But Nut was from Egypt and already married to Geb or Keb and Seb and Thor was from Norway and was married to **Sif** who may or may not have been a nut. Thor did have a great comeback in the sixties. His manager thawed him out and found him steady work running through the pages of Marvel Comics. Sif was not so lucky.

Teacher Tangent #45

Teachers have a tough job when it comes to teaching religion. Some argue that it is best to not let students know what the teacher believes. But many teachers are so talented that they can bring information about their own religion into a classroom without damaging the integrity of any lesson. Teachers also have to be constantly vigilant in case someone is teased for their beliefs. One way to do this is to not ask students to divulge their beliefs. But some students enjoy sharing the name of their belief. What's a teacher to do? I taught in Los Angeles and knew there was great diversity in the classroom and always asked for a show of hands regarding who was Jewish, Muslim, Christian, and even broke it down into the different sects. My point was to show the diversity and we reveled in it. I think if I was in a less diverse situation, I would not call attention to a student's religion. I bring all this up because **sin** is the new entry and in defining it, I don't wish to offend, only teach. I told my students that the state of California expected me to teach lessons in a safe space of learning no matter what one believed, myself included. A key adjective in that last sentence is "safe". I had the kids raise their hands and look around at all the diversity in believing. I wanted them to know they were in an environment where they could thrive safely despite AND because of their differences. I'm still proud of that. By the way, sin is the act of breaking of a religious law. Some sins are crimes, like stealing. Other sins are not crimes, like coveting.

Do you let others **sip** your sodas or do you fret over germs?

Teacher Tangent #46

My father was in the Air Force and I was raised to say "yes **sir**" and "no sir". When I was eighteen, I got my first paying radio job at KQEO in Albuquerque. The boss was David K. Jones and I would say "yes sir" and "no sir" and he'd flinch, telling me to stop. For years, I tried to stop in order to please whomever I was dealing with. I am sure I went years without using it because we have what Robert Bly calls a Sibling Society. He wrote a whole book about it! When my grandfather Sylvester Parsons died in Texas, I remember that he always said "yes sir" and "no sir" and he did so to show respect to whomever he was speaking to and he looked strong saying the words, as if he had chosen them. He had dignity in being respectful and the words came back to me. I've been using them again for more than five years and it sounds good, fits well, and if others have trouble hearing it, so be it.

Do people still use **sis** as a nickname for their sisters? Both my dictionaries say it's okay to do so.

Teachers, don't make your students **sit** too long. Let their blood circulate.

It would be easier to teach if the words that corresponded to numbers had the same number of letters that the word suggests. Shall we count to **six**?

1=n
2=tw
3=tre
4=four

5=phive

6=ssiixx

Of course, we may have trouble when we reach the millions.

**Ska** music began in Jamaica. It is not a bona fide word. But you can dance to it!

I do not **ski**. While skiing, my friend Roger dislocated his shoulder.I also do not rollerblade but I took a lesson and was going to continue when Roger broke his tailbone rollerblading. I was once told we learn through pain but I have evolved enough to learn through Roger's pain.

Where does the **sky** begin? I had forgotten how wonderful that question is until my toddler son asked me to reach up and touch it. We both stretched up and up. I told him that we had reached it. He was quite happy about that.

If you are **sly**, that doesn't mean you're bad. "Sly" is like shrewd or secretly clever. Slyness can be a virtue. But slyness is usually associated with people who trick others and the folks being tricked don't like it much.

My goodness! A word I have never heard of has three entrees! It's another word for our geography dictionary and it is **sny**. A river channel is a sny. So is a certain part of a ship. Our back-up dictionary does not back me up.

To cry very hard is to **sob**.

When planting grass, some people start with seed. Others don't want to wait for it to grow. They want the grass right away so they buy **sod** which has the grass and the ground together.

You can use this one when you know someone's about to pour milk on your cereal and you aren't going to be at the table for a few minutes. Just yell out, "Hey, don't **sog** my flakes!" THE AMERICAN HERITAGE DICTIONARY thinks I'm all wet on this one.

The fifth note on the diatonic scale is **sol**.

I have a **son** and a **daughter**. I am highlighting "daughter" so my girl doesn't think I'm being unfair. Thanks for understanding.

I love to **sop**. To sop is when you have finished eating most of the food on your plate, take a piece of bread, wipe up what's left on the plate, and eat that. Yummy.

Someone who is drunk is a **sot**.

French coins are sometimes called **sou**, pronounced like the name "Sue".

This word has two pronunciations. As a verb, to **sow** is to spread seeds while planting. As a noun, an adult pig is a sow.

The Chicago Cubs have not been to the World Series since 1945. The Chicago White **Sox** haven't been there since 1959. Bonus pain! Both teams lost their last World Series appearance.

Ever tried **soy** milk?

A **spa** is lovely way to be kind to yourself, even if you are a **spy**.

**Sri** is a title of respect in India.

**Stu** Miller was a pitcher for the Giants and Orioles in the sixties. He combined with another pitcher, Steve Barber, to throw a no-hitter but they lost the game! Figure that one out.

A **sty** is a zit on your eyelid. It's a little more gross than a regular pimple because when it pops, the pus goes into your eye!

Teacher Tangent #47

I was a **sub** for nine years in Los Angeles. I loved being a substitute teacher. I taught at many San Fernando Valley elementary schools, especially Roscoe, Dixie Canyon, and Valerio. Of all the jobs I've ever had, subbing was the only one where I knew I was better than most who did it. I reveled at going into classrooms without knowing anyone and having a delightful time shelling out the curriculum. Then a strange thing happened when I was in my mid-thirties. I matured. I was going to a different class every day and realized that it was time for me to establish longer relationships with the students. I dared myself. Be the regular teacher. So I did.

A bubble is one **sud**.

*A Boy Named **Sue*** is sung by Johnny Cash. Did you know it was written by Shel Silverstein? I haven't met a child yet who doesn't laugh at it.

Let's go international! A **suk** is an Arabian marketplace, a measurement for produce in Korea, and when the first letter is capitalized, Suk has to do with a certain kind of people from Nigeria. THE AMERICAN HERITAGE DICTIONARY mentions none of this.

Add two numbers together. The answer is called the **sum**. The sum of three and five is eight.

The **sun** is 93,000,000 miles from Earth.

Your evening meal is called supper in many parts of English speaking areas. To **sup** is to have that meal. Dictionaries don't mention it is also a greeting that has evolved from shortening "What's up?" by people like me who are too lazy to do anything other than nod the head once and barely say one syllable. This word sounds even better while wearing sunglasses.

It's not very often one finds a word that ends with a "q". Do you recall "suk" can be an Arabian marketplace? It can also be spelled s-u-q. **Suq**. Our number two reference chimes in on this entry! But, it does not include "suk"! Words like "suq" make all this research and writing worthwhile.

The number two in German is "zwei". The Australians have taken that and changed it to **swy**. It doesn't exactly mean the number two but it means to be winning by two points. Australia is not in America and therefore, "swy" is not in THE AMERICAN HERITAGE DICTIONARY.

**Syd** Hoff was an artist and an author of children's books. He died in May, 2004.

T

**Tab** is my least favorite soft drink.

A very small amount is a **tad**. Is it bigger than a dab?

In Scotland, **tae** is to.

Teaching a child to **tag** up after the fly is caught is easy. Having the child remember to tag up during the action, especially as the flyball sails through the air, is a whole different ballgame.

Ever had Thai food? My favorite is Rad Na noodles. "Thai" is short for Thailand and THE WORLD BOOK DICTIONARY says **Tai** is an acceptable substitute. THE AMERICAN HERITAGE DICTIONARY agrees. I love it when we all get along.

A **taj** is a type of Muslim cap.

Can you picture a man playing the bagpipes, completely outfitted in his kilt and fancy hat? The hat is called a tam-o'-shanter and **tam** is its nickname.

Is there a difference between beige and **tan**?

**Tao** has two philosophical meanings and two different pronunciations. One is connected to a Chinese philosopher named Confucius and the other is about the moving force of the universe according to Taoists. In the second definition, the first letter is a tee but is pronounced like a dee. *Tao* is also the name of my favorite Rick Springfield album.

**Tap** can mean soft knocking, knocking to make a hole, the hole itself, and even what comes out of the hole.

Used mostly to make roads and other flat surfaces, hot **tar** used to be poured on people! Feathers were added. Thus the phrase, "tarred and feathered".

There are multiple meanings for **tat**. One is about ponies in India. No dictionary provides Tweety Bird's definition for tat.

What is a **tau**? The physicists among us know that it's tiny but weighs three and a half thousand times more than an electron. Tau also refers to a letter in the Greek alphabet.

The last letter in the Hebrew alphabet is **tav** and it can be spelled t-a-u.

Marble players may recognize **taw** as both the name of the game and the line to shoot from.

I said it before and I'll say it again. My mom makes the best iced tea in the world. I don't drink it anymore because I gave up sugar and caffeine. How foolish is that?

In England, a detective is sometimes referred to as a **tec**. Tec does not appear in THE AMERICAN HERITAGE DICTIONARY.

After mowing your lawn, remember to **ted** your clippings.

My first name starts with **tee**.

In Ethiopia, there is a cereal called **tef** which can also be spelled with two effs. THE AMERICAN HERITAGE DICTIONARY recognizes teff but not tef. We'll see this one again in the sequel.

A sheep in its second year, up to the time it is sheared for the first time, is called a **teg**.

When I was fifteen, I played on a football team that won a championship. I was number **ten** and played noseguard. Go Saints!

There is a big celebration every year in Viet Nam called **Tet**.

An obsolete word meaning to work hard is **tew**.

Teacher Tangent #48

**Tex** is not in the dictionary but John Anderson played secondbase for a softball team I was on and he had an accent that placed him far from Los Angeles. Our coach nicknamed him "Tex" and he didn't mind. He will always be in my memory because we won a championship against my old team in the last inning when Tex ran out from the infield and barely caught a weak pop-up with the tying run on third base. Whenever we have lunch, I thank him for his great catch. It saved me a lot of grief.

Shakespeare used such words as thee, thou, and thy. One you'll read less often, but still belongs, is **tha**. THE AMERICAN HERITAGE DICTIONARY which recognizes thee, thou, and thy, doesn't include tha.

There used to be a band called **The** The. There was nothing about The The on the internet when I checked but I just saw their CD in a music store on NW Twenty-Third Street in Portland, Oregon.

Le The **Tho** was a great football player in Viet Nam.

**Thy** means your.

Ever see *Escape From Witch Mountain*? The brother and sister with magical powers are Tony and **Tia**.

A **tic** is a small muscle spasm usually associated with the face.

Please don't get me a **tie** as a present. I rarely have an occasion to wear them.

Do you know that in the game of tag, when you touch someone, that's the verb **tig**? A tig in parts of England is a fight. Tig is not in our second reference dictionary.

You've seen the little wave ~ that goes over some letters in Spanish words. It's called a tilde and it's okay to call it a **til**.

My younger brother's best friend while growing up in Albuquerque was **Tim**. He's a mechanic working on Air Force jets now.

The atomic number of **tin** is fifty.

Uncle in Spanish is **tio**.

A **tip** can be good advice.

There is a tree called a ti. If you have more than one, they would be **tis**, pronounced like "tease". Even though ti is an Asian shrub, it is included in THE AMERICAN HERITAGE DICTIONARY!

There is a small bird called a titmouse. It's considered perfectly acceptable to use just the first syllable when discussing this bird, but if you're in school, use both syllables.

Teacher Tangent #49

Tyr became **Tiu**. Huh? To ancient Norwegians, Tyr was brave enough to put his hand in a wolf's mouth so others could restrain the animal. Tyr got his hand bit off. When the Anglo-Saxons came along, they liked the story but Tyr's name shifted to Tiu. So, big deal right? Old news. Ancient history. Yes, ancient history that comes alive every Tuesday. Tuesday was named after Tiu. The rest of the days? Saturday and Sunday are obvious. Monday is named after the moon. Thursday is Thor's day. Friday is named after Fria. Go learn about Wednesday, I've done enough.

There are farmers in central Nigeria known as **Tiv**. That's also the name of their language.

**Tiz** is a European singer-songwriter hoping to make the big time.

In parts of Africa, a **tob** is a long garment made of cotton. THE AMERICAN HERITAGE DICTIONARY does not include this entry.

British slang for being alone is **tod**. THE AMERICAN HERITAGE DICTIONARY has two totally different definitions. It is a bona fide word.

I have never understood the **toe** game, *This Little Piggy Goes To Market*, despite playing it thousands of times.

Teacher Tangent #50

I had a roommate named Bernard. He spoke two words so well that I tried to bring them into my vocabulary. Bernard called a car "ride" and any kind of clothing was "threads". I tried to copy Bernard but couldn't make it work. Perhaps I will have better luck with **tog**. Togs are clothes, I mean, threads.

**Tom** is a great American name. There's Tom Sawyer, Tom Seaver, and Tom Foolery.

Two thousand pounds is a **ton**.

Teacher Tangent #51

**Too** means also. It has another meaning, too. It can mean more than is needed. I love to use music to teach children, hoping that melodies get stuck in their head and helps them retain info that otherwise would have to be cleaned up from the floor. I always wanted to bring out Elvis Presley's *Too Much* to show the kids an example of "too" that they would easily recall. I never used the song because it had to do with being obsessed with a girl and did not feel appropriate. But this tune DOES help convey the "more than is needed" definition of too.

Teacher Tangent #52

In 1975, while I was living in Athens, Greece, the radio announcer on American Forces Radio played *Top Of The World* by the Carpenters. His name was Lovable Lou Jackson. I memorized what he said because it sounded so slick: "I'm on Top of the World with four pennies in my pocket and a polar bear at my side. You can't beat that, baby!" Years later, when I was a radio announcer on KQEO, I said exactly the same thing for the same song but couldn't pull off the same coolness as Sgt. Lou Jackson.

A hill with lots of rocks is a **tor**. BOTH dictionaries have it!

Does anyone still call a small child a **tot**? It's acceptable.

**Tow** trucks. Enough said.

Does receiving a new **toy** ever equal the desire for it?

A trimaran is a sailing vessel. It doesn't tip easily because instead of one main body (called a hull), there are three hulls. A trimaran can be called a **tri**. You can get a fancy one for around seven hundred dollars. Our back-up dictionary argues the first three letters of "trimaran" are a prefix and not a word unto itself.

Abraham Lincoln is the best example of someone who would **try** again after failing.

When my two kids are in the **tub**, they don't want to get out.

My favorite Paul McCartney album is ***Tug of War***. I love the song he sang for John Lennon called *Here Today*. It feels like he quietly let me into the chemistry of their relationship, mixed with the sadness of losing Mr. Lennon.

There is a type of bird from New Zealand called a **tui**.

If my stomach is upset, I take a couple of Tums. But what if I only take one? That would be a Tum, right? No, **tum** is not a word.

A **tun** is a barrel of alcohol, a measure of nearly 252 gallons of liquid, or the 360 days that the Mayans viewed as a solar year.

A male ram can also be called a **tup**.

Begin a sentence with **tut** if you are mildly annoyed.

A question a man considers at some point in his life is whether to rent or buy a **tux**. Most men, like me, are renters. I have only had to wear a tuxedo about half a dozen times. Which reminds me, I better take them back.

Two in Scotland is **twa**.

In Ghana, there is a tribe and a language known as **twi**, which rhymes with "tree".

There are a lot of good **two** songs, here are two: *Two Hearts Beat As One* by U2 and *Two Fine People* by Cat Stevens.

Did you know Martin and **Twy** got married? I wasn't invited either.

What is a **tyg**? It's a cup with at least two handles so that different people can drink from different places on the rim! I'm serious. The Jamestown Museum has a web site with some pictures. The origin of the word is uncertain. THE AMERICAN HERITAGE DICTIONARY does not include this word.

**Tyr** became Tiu. Tyr is a God from Norse mythology. Is this another deja vu?

U

Uncle **Ubb** is a character in <u>Dr.Seuss's ABC</u>

**Uda** Walawe is a park in Sri Lanka.

In Japan and China there is a plant called an **udo** and part of it is edible.

It's interjection time! **Ugh** means, among other things, you've bitten into chocolate candy with insides not to your liking.

An informal way of saying ukulele is **uke**.

Is **ulu** a word? Yep. It's an eskimo knife. THE AMERICAN HERITAGE DICTIONARY cuts out "ulu" but the internet has web sites about ulu knives and even one about the ulu fruit tree of Hawaii.

Don't mess with **Uma** Thurman.

An umpire can be called an **ump**. Mostly, I believe they are called "blue" because of the color of their shirts. In Rochester, New York, I saw umps in red shirts. They were still called blue.

One in Spanish is **uno** and *Uno* is a great card game.

"Up" can be an adverb, adjective, verb, and noun. Since it can be a noun, that means it can conceivably exist as a plural, therefore, **ups** makes the three letter word team.

A city is an urban area and can also be called an **urb**. Our back-up claims it is only a prefix.

In India, **urd** is a bean. In Norse mythology, Urd is the goddess of fate. In our back-up, urd is nothing.

Midge **Ure** is a musician who has made a lot of CD's. He was a member of Ultravox.

**Uri** is a Hebrew name.

After death, some bodies get put into the ground, others are dropped into the sea and still others have their body cremated. The ashes that remain after cremation are placed in an **urn** until they are scattered over a special place.

David **Ury** is an actor and a comedian.

I hope you put this book to good **use**.

**Uta** Hagen was an actress and an extraordinary acting teacher.

Utah was named after the **Ute** Indians.

An **uzi** is a type of machine gun.

V

In West Africa, a **Vai** is a member of the Mandingo people. It is also the name of the language.

**Val** Kilmer was okay as Batman. I think Elvis, in his prime, would have been a great Batman.

A **van** can also be the front part of an approaching army. May you never see one.

An acronym taken from the first letters of volt, ampere, and reactive is **var**, which is a unit of measuring reactive power. THE AMERICAN HERITAGE DICTIONARY pulled the plug on this entry.

The vascular system is the blood and how it moves through your body. Your veins are blood vessels that carry blood all through you. Another word for vessels is **vas**.

Is it me or do all the quotation marks in this book look like we spilled a **vat** of glitter? Yes, I know vats usually contain liquids. Obviously, you've never seen a first grader mixing his glue with glitter and turning an entire art project into liquid.

The sixth letter of the Hebrew alphabet is **vav**.

Teacher Tangent #53

I ask my friends when they were born. They always tell me. I skip over to Joel Whitburn's Top Pop Singles 1955-1996. I stop skipping and look up the Number One song in the USA the day they were born. For example, my brother Dusty was born when *Come Together* by the Beatles was Number One. The most synchronistic song matching a birth belongs to Mark Talgo. On the day he entered the world, the Number One song was *Take Good Care of My Baby* by Bobby Vee. **Vee** is also the word for "v".

A relatively new word, **veg** is the mindless act of relaxing.

"Oy **veh**!" is a great Jewish expression. It is Hebrew, not English.

This one is short for two entirely different multisyllabic nouns. A **vet** is an animal doctor. It's short for veterinarian. Vet is also short for veteran, a former soldier. After the leaving the army, the vet went to school to become a vet.

To annoy or disturb someone is to **vex** them.

The definition of **via** is "by way of". It answers the question of how something is going to happen. I am going uptown via the bus.

A guy named **Vic** has owed my dad money for more than twenty-five years!

You have heard of the spelling rule, "change the y to i and add the suffix" for such words as "fly" and "satisfy", which can become "flies" and "satisfied". Well, **vie** is a verb that is the root word of "vies" but it also can become "vying", where the aforementioned rule is turned on its head. To vie is to compete.

In the 60's, a song called *Love Will Make You Fail In School* was released on **Vik** Records.

To feel great and ready for anything is **vim**.

I've never seen a **Vin** Diesel movie. I guess he won't be endorsing this book.

A Latin word for power is **vis**. THE AMERICAN HERITAGE DICTIONARY does not have "vis" but does mention the island of Vis. Is Vis near Latin? Okay...enough. Let's play straight. There is no country called Latin, Latinland, Latintown, Latinopia, Latinopolos, Latinberg, or Latin. But ordinary ancient Romans spoke Vulgar Latin. As the Roman Empire crumbled, Vulgar Latin broke down into what we call the Romance Languages. The four languages that evolved from Vulgar Latin are Spanish, Portuguese, French, and Italian. It sure is fun to mention "vulgar" so often in an academic setting! What did you say? No, this is not a tangent. You should KNOW at least something basic about Latin. Not knowing is vulgar. Of course, I just learned it myself at verbix.com. How did I graduate from college without knowing that?

My dad's Aunt Vivian was my great aunt. She was always very good to me and would send me newspaper articles about Nolan Ryan while I was growing up. I miss her. I always called her Aunt Vivian but someone along the way must have called her **Viv**.

**Viz** is a publisher of manga stories.


Teacher Tangent #54

I bet this is the longest paragraph in any book anywhere devoted to this topic. The entry is **vly**. It's not very often use you see those three letters together in a row. "Vly" means "vlei". What's a vlei? A vlei is a vley. It is also acceptable to use "vlaie". All of these have to do with a gathering of water larger than a pond but smaller than a lake. To make it more confusing, that definition only applies to South Africa. In the United States, all these spellings refer to a swamp or a marsh. Just when I thought it was all figured out, THE WORLD BOOK DICTIONARY mentions that it can also mean "creek", which suggests moving water, unlike a swamp or marsh. How can such a versatile word never get used? The movie *Swamp Thing* might be scarier if it was *Vly Thing*. Would *Dawson's Creek* have been successful if it had been named *Dawson's Vly*? THE AMERICAN HERITAGE DICTIONARY winds away from the issue by saying nothing of vly, vlei, or vley. I wonder why.


Another word for the Geography Dictionary! Aren't you glad you saved yours? A narrow inlet of the sea is a **voe**. The man who wrote The Jungle Book was Rudyard Kipling. He used "voe" in his work. THE AMERICAN HERITAGE DICTIONARY does not include voe but the three letter combo does live on in the Shetland Islands at a narrow inlet called *Sullom Voe*.

189

**Vog** is a new acronym about air pollution from volcanoes but it is not a bona fide word.

Let's meet for lunch in **Voh**, New Caledonia.

In some German names, **von** is used between the first and last name to suggest someone's place in the caste system. It can mean "of" or "from". THE AMERICAN HERITAGE DICTIONARY does not include von but does give a good entry for Kurt Vonnegut, Jr. He is one of my favorite writers.

A **vow** is a promise.

Kenny Loggins has a CD called *Vox Humana*, which means human voice. The best song on that album is a long one called *Love Will Follow*. It's the last track. In THE AMERICAN HERITAGE DICTIONARY, "vox" is not listed by itself. It is entered with "vox angelica" and "vox humana". They must like the Kenny Loggins record, too.

It's not a word but my wife drives a Saturn **Vue**.

A hole in a rock in the mining industry is called a **vug**.

Teacher Tangent #55

I was born in Austin, Texas. When I was two, my family moved to Izmir, Turkey. We came back when I was six and went quickly from Mankato, Minnesota to San Antonio, Texas to Washington DC where I stayed until the beginning of third grade when we went back to Mankato, Minnesota. The next year, 1970, we went to Albuquerque, New Mexico for four years and Athens, Greece for four more years. When I was eighteen, my folks bought a house in Albuquerque where my parents still live. I lived in Los Angeles for sixteen years and now reside in Portland, Oregon. Now, on page 2348, which, coincidentally, is the year I plan to STOP moving so much, THE WORLD BOOK DICTIONARY suggests that in the United States, there is a dialect that uses **vum** as a word to mean promise, the way vow means promise. I never heard it. But I haven't lived in New England. Yet. THE AMERICAN HERITAGE DICTIONARY says that "vum" is "an alteration of the word vow that goes all the way back to the American Revolution."[2] Whoa.

W

A web in Scotland is a **wab**.

[2] Copyright 2000 by Houghton Mifflin Company. Adapted and reproduced by permission from THE AMERICAN HERITAGE DICTIONARY OF THE ENGLISH LANGUAGE, FOURTH EDITION.

A lot of paper money in your hand is a **wad** of cash. You may start with a stick of gum but once it's in your mouth, it's a wad. Wad can also be a verb. Ever started writing and made a frustrating mistake? Just wad the paper up and toss it! Don't hit anyone. If you miss the recycling bin, get up, and try again.

Woe is sadness. But wait, we're not there yet so here's an obsolete synonym: **wae**. Delinquent readers will be happy to know that there is also an entry for "waesucks". If you use it in the near future and someone gives you a hard time about your grammar, just whip out your handy-dandy WORLD BOOK DICTIONARY and if it's the 1987 edition, turn to page 2349, and point it out. By the way, it's an interjection so it's okay to shout it out. Make sure it's THE WORLD BOOK DICTIONARY you are holding because our number two source knows better than to include obsolete words.

Teacher Tangent #56

My mom was a **WAF**, which was an acronym for a woman in the Air Force. It is no longer used. My mom worked in the Pentagon and in Newfoundland back in the fifties. She grew up in a small town in Iowa and joined the Air Force to see the world. She still remembers the excitement of getting on the train in Iowa in 1952 and bounding out for her future. I am grateful I was a part of it.

You thought **wag** was a verb but it can also be a noun to describe a jokester, the class clown, or a goofy teacher.

Synonyms of **wan** are pale and barely. The entry on page 2355 of THE WORLD BOOK DICTIONARY gets poetic by using "the wan sunlight of winter". Can you see that image?

To **wap** something is to hit it.

Teacher Tangent #57
The following quotes about **war** were spoken by wiser and braver folks than me.

Dwight Eisenhower was both a soldier (he was a general) and a President. He said, "I think that people want peace so much that one of these days government had better get out of their way and give it to them."

Ulysses Grant was also a general and a President. He said, "There never was a time when, in my opinion, some way could not be found that to prevent the drawing of the sword."

John Kennedy, a Naval officer and a President, said, "Mankind must put an end to war,before war puts an end to mankind."

According to THE WORLD BOOK DICTIONARY, it used to be good grammar to use "you **was**" in a sentence but it's no longer that way. I wish it hadn't changed because so many students still use it. Seems like accepting it as good grammar is easier than correcting so many students who aren't going to change saying "you was" anytime soon.

In Ethiopia, there is a spicy stew called **wat**.

Pop quiz: What's the sixth letter of the Hebrew alphabet? Hint: Look back in the vee's. Go ahead, this is an open book test. That's right! Vav! Vav can also be called **waw**. Wow.

The good news is my dad taught me how to **wax** a car. The bad news is that he had more than one car and sometimes there were trucks. The best news is that, now, whenever I wash or wax my car, I feel the connection to him and my brothers and hear the phrases my dad would tell us while we worked. "Tanner, why don't you rinse your shammy and get the windows?" He wasn't really asking.

When Elvis Presley died, he had a hit single on the Top 40 charts. The song was *Way Down* and it was on an album made of blue vinyl!

There was a Native American tribe from Indiana called **Wea**. It was a strong tribe. According to their web site, they have been gathering again and they have close to two hundred members. I hope they grow enough to be recognized in the next edition of THE AMERICAN HERITAGE DICTIONARY. It will give added meaning to the word "heritage".

THE WORLD BOOK DICTIONARY, which has served us so well, has thirteen definitions for **web** but, since it is the 1987 edition, has nothing about the worldwide web. I grew up without a computer. My parents grew up without TV. Your children will have things as yet unimagined.

To **wed** someone is to marry them.

You thought **wee** was what to yell while snowboarding but it really means small. It's tinier than tiny.

**Wei** Liu is the author of <u>Biking Out</u>.

Ever had a **wen**? Near as I can tell, it's a zit on your scalp.

A wergild is the price of money paid to a family in Germany by someone who is caught committing a crime against that family. The short term is **wer**. THE AMERICAN HERITAGE DICTIONARY has "wer"!

**Wes** Parker was a great fielding firstbaseman for the Dodgers.

I live in Portland, Oregon where it's frequently **wet**.

Who started putting the silent "gh" in words? English is difficult enough to spell already. "Weigh" should be **wey**. In fact, "wey" is a word and wouldn't you know it? It's a unit of weight. Now, measurement units are supposed to agree so everyone can get the math correct but in England, where weys are weighed, there are several variations of how much a wey weighs. THE AMERICAN HERITAGE DICTIONARY does not weigh in on wey.

I have always enjoyed participating in the *Who's On First?* routine. It's a skit in the public domain and practicing it with a friend is a great way to see if you like doing comedy.

In South Central Los Angeles, they have some fantastic **wig** stores with hundreds of wigs.

**Wil** can play basketball intensely and carry on a conversation simultaneously.

I am grateful when my perception of a **win**-lose scenario is altered to a win-win scenario. It's a matter of faith, attitude, and slowing down my breathing.

The English of a thousand years ago is called "Old English". Back then, one could say **wis** and everyone would know the meaning was "to know". A millennium later, "wis" comes back, showing itself in this little book, looking bewildered after its long sleep, wondering how to work its way back into the lingo.

To be a **wit** is not only to be funny but it is to be smart funny. Toilet humor can be funny but never witty. Wit is sharper than clever.

A **wiz** is not only smart but fast smart.

Teacher Tangent #58

I love Robert Bly's writing. He writes poetry and social commentary. He is of the opinion that one of the things we need to do in our culture is grieve. Perhaps some of us are sad and don't know it. People can grieve in different ways but crying, sobbing, weeping are the main ways we grieve. Oh, the point of the paragraph; another word for sadness is **woe**. Do you know any tales of woe? Shakespeare wrote <u>Romeo and Juliet</u>. In the opening he mentions that it is the greatest tale of woe ever! Such boldness! I auditioned for the part of Romeo but landed the much smaller part of Paris. I wasn't happy not being the star but a funny thing happened because the director had once played Paris and gave me the best direction I ever got as an actor. For the those of you don't know, Paris was engaged to Juliet and in most productions he is portrayed as a rich brat, sort of like Draco Malfoy, and the audience sees him as another obstacle in Romeo's pursuit of Juliet; in other words, a bad guy. Well, director Benjamin Lamb made me play Paris as a perfect man who was very happy to be wedding Juliet. Paris was a smart and refined man who was a great catch for any maiden but he got caught up in the nutty business of being naive to sneaky love and obsession and paid for it with his life. Ben Lamb taught me that when characters are strong and full of good intentions and actions, then tragedy is even greater in the end. The proof that he loved Juliet is in the scene where he goes to her grave at night to profess his feelings. A rich brat wouldn't have bothered to share such woe. Romeo, brat that he is, listens in on Paris saying nice things to Juliet's tomb and gets so angry, he duels Paris and kills him. As Romeo holds the dead Paris, Romeo cries. For a moment, he realizes the insidiousness of his obsession. He's killed someone as noble as Paris. It was a small part and I was truly challenged because I'm quite imperfect. My director said I did a good job, but he did the better one. He gave the good direction which gave the audience more reason to cry. The moral of my tale is worth repeating. When you tell a story, make everyone a good guy so when the bad things happen, it hurts worse, it makes the reader grieve. Shakespeare and Bly would agree with that.

In Australia, a **wog** is any small germ or insect.

Fresh vegetables cooked in a **wok** is good eating!

The last two baseball games I played in, we **won**.

When someone is attracted to someone else and is trying to get their attention, that is the verb **woo**. After people get married, one of the hard parts is remembering to woo the other person from time to time.

A synonym for hit is whop. THE WORLD BOOK DICTIONARY says **wop** equals whop but our back-up doesn't include this definition. Jon Mersel wants everyone to stop hitting.

How absurd, **wot** is a word.

Children can be naughty and witty at the same time! Certain adults recognize this and are **wry** about it. To be wry is to give a smile saluting the cleverness while at the same time passing along a dirty look that reminds children not to be so silly. The best wry smile belongs to Chris Biblarz. She adds a slow movement of the head downward that wins the prize.

In our house, WUD stands for Weird Uncle Dave who is very good at sending postcards to his nephew and his niece. But, as a word, **wud** is a dud. Except in Scotland, where wud is wood.

Y starts with a W. Yep, **wye** is Y. Both of my dictionaries agree. Shockingly, "wye" is also a piece of electrical equipment.

Y

I mean wye.

Wait. Where's x? I mean ex? No three letter words start with ex and I don't want to be one of those lame alphabet books which dig and dig for some nutty ex reference. In this book, ex is axed.

My friend Roger, who is busy illustrating the cover, (it is difficult to type these words while he keeps trying to paint the front) reminds me that his favorite band, **XTC**, is only three letters long and I remind him that I don't include abbreviations.

Back to Y.

I mean wye.

A laser beam is generated by a **YAG**. Our primary reference does not mention wye, I mean, why, all three letters in YAG are upper case. It does mention that it was named after a Japanese electrical engineer named Hidetsugu Yagi.

It's interjection time! My grandfather said **yah** when he meant "yeah". This is because he had a Norwegian accent. Apparently, though, "yah" is a brother to other negative interjections like "pooh" and "bah". The people who wrote THE AMERICAN HERITAGE DICTIONARY, probably think this is crazy talk.

The ox of central Asia and Tibet is the **yak**.

**Yal** is an album of North African music by an artist named Takfarinas.

A **yam** is a vegetable. Eat more of them.

**Yao** Ming is a basketball player from China. Also in China, there is a Yao nationality, which is a group of people. In Japan, there is a city named Yao. Yao Ming, by the way, is a Virgo.

A **yap** can refer not only to loud talking but also to the mouth it's coming from.

To be active and nimble and quick is to be yare and **yar** is also acceptable. So ther. THE AMERICAN HERITAGE DICTIONARY mentions "yare" but says nothing about "yar". So there.

You've gone in a straight line and then turned unknowingly. Well, that action is to **yaw** and it finds usage in the boat and plane businesses.

**Yaz** is both an 80's band and a nickname for Carl Yastrzemski of the Red Sox.

Yeah is the lazy yes but **yea** is yes in voting and in expressing a truth.

Some folks have gone to all the trouble of naming the celestial stars around us. Two of them are **Yed** Posterior and Yed Prior. Don't ask me to point them out.

Danny **Yee** is a book reviewer in Australia. Well, Mr. Yee, how am I doing?

John Bruce **Yeh** plays the clarinet for the Chicago Symphony Orchestra.

Japanese money is **yen** but it is also a verb that means to desire something. A synonym for yen is yearn.

Douglas **Yeo** plays trombone for the Boston Symphony Orchestra.

**Yep** feels like a yes that comes from a man wearing overalls.

**Yes**, we're almost done!

But not **yet**.

There is an evergreen tree called a **yew**.

**Yia** Yang is a bus driver in St. Paul, Minnesota.

**Yid** Vicious is a Wisconsin band that plays traditional Yiddish music.

Su-Jin **Yim** is a writer for the Oregonian.

There is an Asian philosophy that deals with **yin** and yang. Yin is the dark side with the small white dot.

**Yio** Chu Kang is a city in Singapore.

A dog's bark can be called a **yip**. It's bona fide.

**Yma** Sumac, born in Peru, had a #1 album in the 50's. She was also on Broadway.

There are boys who are rude and not nice. In England, such a boy might be called a **yob**. Notice that yob is boy spelled backwards, which has to do with the origination of the word.

The tenth letter of the Hebrew alphabet is **yod**.

**Yoh** Asakura sleeps in class!

In Judaism, **Yom** Kippur is a day of atonement.

Yonder can mean there. Where are my car keys? Over yonder. Shakespeare used it when he had Romeo say, "What light through yonder window breaks?" which means, "Who turned the light on in that room over there?" Well, **yon** is an archaic short form of "yonder".

Teacher Tangent #59

**You** has got to be the most popular word in pop music titles. *You and Me, You and I, You Are So Beautiful, You Are Everything, You Send Me, You Light Up My Life, You Should Be Dancing, You Might Think, You Won't See Me.* All this finger pointing and control! Nine different times there has been a song simply titled *You* that has hit the charts. The most popular one being by George Harrison back in 1975. It was from his album *Extra Texture* and I still remember Mike Nibi walking out of the store and showing me that orange cover when it was brand new.

Ever barked like a dog or meowed like a cat? That action is a **yow**, pronounced like you.

**Yub** is an Ewok word, not an English one.

**Yud** is a Hebrew letter.

When discovering the milk has gone bad, **yuk** is an appropriate response. There are plenty of inappropriate responses.

Yummy and yum-yum are words but **yum** is not? How can that be?

Another lazy form of yes is **yup**.

Watase **Yuu** is an anime artist.

Heero **Yuy** is an anime character.

**Yuz** Aleshkovsky is an obscure writer. I should talk!

Z

I mean zee.

**Zab** Judah is a professional boxer.

Is it possible to **zag** without zigging?

**Zam** is a character in the Star Wars universe.

When lightning strikes, that's **zap**. "Zap", like "Pow" and "Bap", is a word they flashed on the screen during the fights in the old *Batman* TV show. Zap can also mean quickness.

**Zav**, a former student, always rises to an academic challenge and he can tell a joke well.

A special tool in the roofing business is a **zax**.

When I started this book, I guessed that z-e-e was the correct way to spell "z". I was right, but only in the United States. The British use the word **zed** to mean **zee**. I don't make this up. Nor did I make up "zax".

There is Buddhism and **Zen** Buddhism. I don't know the difference but I think zen refers to meditation. Don't quote me!

Los Angeles County Supervisor **Zev** Yaroslavsky has lived his whole life in the district he represents.

Do you recall back in the dee's there was an animal called a dzo that was the cross between the water buffalo and the yak? Me neither. THE WORLD BOOK DICTIONARY claims a **zho** is the same thing. THE AMERICAN HERITAGE DICTIONARY has no zho. Perhaps they think zhos are extinct. I saw a picture of a zho once. Honest.

The **Zia** tribe is in New Mexico and their sun sign is on the state flag.

Can you **zig** without zagging?

Stanley **Zin** is a Bobby Orr fan.

Which is faster, a **zip** or a zap?

A pimple is a **zit**. So is a wen.

A "zoon" is a fancy zoological term having to do with being a complete organism. I think it's plural is **zoa**.

General **Zod** is an evil villain in Superman II.

**Zoe** is my neighbor.

**Zon** Guitars are made in Redwood City, California. I hope you remember that all the proper names we've been using are not bona fide words.

Teacher's Last Tangent
My mom considers any room with more than three people a **zoo**. No matter where she's been, she'll tell you it was a zoo. When I go to the real zoo, I love to say, "This place is a zoo!" No one laughs the first time I say it or any of the subsequent times but I entertain myself with my mother's accent for hours.

Victor **Zue** is a professor at MIT. People there can write books about fifteen and twenty letter words!

Peter J. **Zug** is a legislator in Pennsylvania.

Inon **Zur** composed music for *Power Rangers Turbo*.

*Zus* & *Zo* is a movie from 2003. Never zaw it.

An archaic Hebrew coin is a **zuz**.

Here are more obscure bands: Dr. **Zog**, **Zox**, **zua** neken, **zYc**, **Zie**, **Zyg**, and **Zyn**.

Before *The Mighty Morphin Power Rangers*, there were *The Zyu Rangers*.

For homework, I look forward to hearing how you've incorporated many of these easy words into your daily activities. Worry not. Nothing is due. Are they working on the bells today? They should ring now. No, you cannot be dismissed early. Don't cry about it. Would you mind though if I drop some tears?

These tears are because my brilliant idea ended with a list of obscure musical acts and a double mention of *The Power Rangers*.

I am crying because one of you skipped the lecture and ran all the way here to the ending just to see how it all turns out. Well, nobody died. Now go back and read the boring parts.

I'm blubbering on because you won't listen to any of the music I have suggested, insisting that your music is better. Give different music a chance. Try jazz. Try mariachi. Don't be just a rapper, metal head, reggae jammer, lounge lizard, cowboy, or a slow dancer. Try them all. It will help you be a lifelong learner.

I am sobbing because I am my own editor. All the mistakes are mine. A writer editing his own work is similar to an alleged criminal being his own attorney. It's like cutting your own hair. Point out my mistakes at misterparsons@earthlink.net. I'm sure you'll let me know any three letter combinations I forgot to include. Perhaps your name is Xyq and you were in my class but I've forgotten. Complain. I understand.

I am truly sad because you are growing within a violent culture that I cannot stop.

If I had it all to do over again, I would have flunked all of my students so that we could stay together for years in one very crowded classroom. I miss my students. But, like Holden Caulfield, I cannot catch you as you fall. I'm crying because, the mere fact that I teach means I help push you over the edge. The best that I can do is make you laugh. Okay, I taught the curriculum well but I should have focused more on courtesy, compassion, and tolerance. When is that bell going to ring?

Okay, here's the truth. You taught me more than I ever taught you. When I started teaching, I was a substitute thrilled with making one hundred dollars a day. I had no idea what I was doing in the classroom. I wanted to be a movie star but there were enough of those. Some people teach because it is a calling. For me, it was a dragging. Principals liked that I showed up on time, taught from the books, and let kids express joy. It was you who constantly, every single minute of every hour of every day; it was you who showed me courtesy, compassion, and tolerance when I was there happy to make my hundred bucks and get home by three-thirty for a nap. You taught me. Never forget that. The bell tolls for thee. Please straighten your desk and make sure your area is clean before you leave.

# Acknowledgments

To make this like a movie experience, please hold this page about belt high and slowly move it up the way credits roll at the end of a film. Play a song by Missing Persons called *Words* for the soundtrack.

You think you've got problems? Steve Duin has three essays due every week! He writes a newspaper column for the Oregonian. He makes brave and bold points with clear and strong language. I am honored that he wrote the foreword for this book.

Janet Peterson at World Book Publishing gave me permission to quote from THE WORLD BOOK DICTIONARY. She wants me to remind you that it's best to quote from the most recent edition.

Brianne Lutfy, the gatekeeper at Houghton Mifflin, gave permission to quote from THE AMERICAN HERITAGE DICTIONARY OF THE ENGLISH LANGUAGE: FOURTH EDITION.

Roger Shank drew the cover illustration. Clap for him.

Elena Frank, Roclyn Gallet, Peter Joyes, Bonnie McLean, Alma & Olivia Siulagi, and Becca Sutton graciously read early drafts. Alma gave excellent notes.

Thanks to the entire staff at the Garden Home Community Library for support and being good to my children. Thanks also to Cynthia Bond, Jessica Drake-Young, Bruce Gelfand, Duane Hansen & The Mac Store, Cheri LaRochelle, The Mersel Family, Patricia O'Connor, Mr. Rains, Benjamin Schick, Solos3, Mark Talgo, Mia Wall, and my parents, who've been married longer than Elvis has been famous.

The Westside Writers actually did all the work but let me take credit for it.

LAUSD was kind enough to employ me for many years. UTLA provided extraordinary support for me as a teacher.

My wife Tracey contributed all things beyond words. My preschool son and baby daughter helped by taking over the laundry, gardening, and keeping the house immaculate so Daddy could finish.

# Bibliography

The American Heritage Dictionary of the English Language, Fourth
Edition
Copyright 2000 by Houghton Mifflin utilized via bartleby.com

Joel Whitburn's Top Pop Singles 1955-1996
Copyright 1997 by Record Research Inc.

The Oxford Shakespeare
Edited by W.J. Craig
London: Oxford University Press 1914
New York: Bartleby.com 2000

Oh Say Can You Say By Dr. Seuss
Copyright 1979 by Dr. Seuss Enterprise
Random House Inc. New York

The Sports Encyclopedia: Baseball 1994 Edition by David S. Neft
& Richard M. Cohen
Copyright 1994 St. Martin's Press New York

THE WORLD BOOK DICTIONARY 1987 Edition
Copyright 1987 by Doubleday & Company Inc.

I got permission to adapt and reproduce quotes for:

Nine definitions from <u>THE WORLD BOOK DICTIONARY</u>.

Copyright World Book, Inc.

By permission of the publisher. www.worldbook.com


I also used brainydictionary.com, brainyquote.com, Google.com, and baseball-reference.com

# Outtakes

Rolling...Kiss has a song called **I**. Beyonce sings *Me Myself & I*. There is a Beatle song CUT. Hey, too many songs. Can we shorten it up?

**Anx** is not a word? It's a combination of guilt, worry, and shame! No? It's not anybody's name? Get the phonebook! Fine. Let's move on. Are we having food delivered?

Rolling...Take Thirteen...Here is a perfect examplth...wait....keep rolling....Here is a prefect eggshample....no no, let's keep it going.... I'll get it.

Rolling....CUT! You gotta tell me when something is hanging from my nose!

Before we roll on this one, are we sure **Ned** throws the greatest knucklecurve with a whiffleball in the entire universe? How do we know? We did? We tested everyone on the planet and everyone on all the other planets? We didn't miss one person? Good enough for me.

Rolling....When discovering the milk has gone bad, #*&@! is appropriate. CUT! What? Oh, yes, I forgot the **yuk**. What? This is an outtake! I'm supposed to curse! Okay, let's do a clean one.

In Britain, the last letter is **zee**. In the USA, the last letter is **zed**. Aww---nuts. It's the other way around. I'm not doing it again. Just keep it. Think anyone will notice?

# About The Author

Tanner Parsons is the most fortunate man on Earth. He lives in utter luxury with the three people he loves the most. He smiles and laughs a lot. He likes to tease everyone he meets. Whining and complaining are his worst habits but he's working to overcome them. His first book, **Baseball Summer**, is available at amazon.com. This is his second book. His third is complete but the words are out of order. He will skip the fourth book in order to begin working on his fifth one. Now, go to sleep.

Printed in the United States
20823LVS00002BA/55-156